HOPE GREW ROUND *Me*

A daughter's life-threatening accident plants the seeds of a mother's self-discovery

BARB GREENBERG

Julie —
Hope always
love,
Barb

Beaver's Pond Press, Inc.
Edina, Minnesota

ISBN 1-59298-064-3

Library of Congress Catalog Number: 2004104919

Book design and typesetting: Mori Studio
Cover design: Mori Studio

Printed in the United States of America

First Printing: April 2004

07 06 05 04   6 5 4 3 2 1

Beaver's Pond Press, Inc.

7104 Ohms Lane, Suite 216
Edina, MN 55439
(952) 829-8818
www.BeaversPondPress.com

To order, visit www.BookHouseFulfillment.com or call
1-800-901-3480. Reseller and special sales discounts available.

Dedicated to

Bessie Hope, Ann Getzug,

and Joe Weitzman

ACKNOWLEDGEMENTS

Roxy Lerner who innocently asked, "Have you ever written anything?" Marly Rusoff for encouraging me, even when it was clear I had no idea what I was doing. Audrey D'le Marte and Cindy Rogers, my editors, for their gentle voices and loving guidance.

Lorraine Link, our angel. The first in the series that saved our daughter's life. Dr. D'urso, our hero, who, along with the amazing men and women of the Royal Brisbane Hospital, used their medical and technical excellence with energy, intensity, and heart. Medical staff from Hervey Bay to Brisbane to Minneapolis: ambulance drivers, helicopter pilots, doctors, nurses, therapists, social workers. You are all part of making our miracle happen.

Each person who sent a card or a prayer, phoned, or e-mailed: You made a difference. Barry Strickland and the staff at the Gregory Terrace who adopted us as family and gave us a home when we felt so homeless. The Jasons, who became family though we have never met. My Mary Kay family and mentors, beautiful inside and out. My Byerly's service counter buddies.

Peggy Sacco for your wise counsel. Ann Gosack for encouraging me to ride, and Lainie DeBoer, for her patience when I did ride. Margaret Roth, for sharing Sparky. Sunshine Epstein, wherever you are. Stevie Q., our favorite solicitor. Bev Smiley for your magic touch. Peg Cowart, typist and computer whiz extraordinaire. Jenny Dirkes for coming to my rescue.

Shira and Ilana, my blessings, my inspiration.

CHAPTER

One

June 14, 2000 Minneapolis

I'm scared. Always and about everything.

Driving down the freeway on a hot June morning, the headache I'd managed to control for the past three days leaked down my back and into my shoulders. My death grip on the steering wheel didn't help the tension in my body, but the traffic zipping by me was too close and too fast, and I was certain that my slightest wrong move would be deadly.

Today's test of my worth on this dangerous outing was to get all my errands done before I met Ann for lunch. Had I told the shoe repairman the wrong thing about fixing my boots? It turned out I had. One black mark.

I picked up Mickey's dry cleaning, paid the girl, and walked back out to my car, leaving his suit still hanging by the counter. Two black marks.

I rushed back in, caught my purse in the door, broke the strap, grabbed the suit, and ran out again. Three black marks.

I was late getting to the restaurant. Four black marks.

I caught my reflection in the glass door and saw that my hair had exploded into an uncontrolled mass of dark curls because I hadn't taken the time to blow it dry earlier in the morning. Five black marks.

With this many mistakes, something awful could happen again. If only I could be better, there would be no more danger and my family might be safe.

Lunch with Ann helped. She loved me, black marks and all. We'd met years before at a horse show, two nervous amateurs each waiting anxiously on a hot dusty afternoon for our turn to enter the ring and gallop our horses over a course of eight jumps, hoping not to embarrass ourselves too terribly and as an afterthought, not to hurt ourselves either. She'd seen me with a lot more than five black marks over the years. At a horse show, I could accumulate mistakes faster than I could get bucked off into the nearest manure pile.

At the restaurant, Ann welcomed me with a strong hug and we settled into our booth. Not interested in any whimpy salads, we each ordered large bowls of pasta. Ann listened to my story, the one I couldn't tell over the phone because there was too much. Her big brown eyes blinked back tears, and then she began to swear. Her language was brilliant. Simple but brilliant. The clear, bright, sharp anger refreshed me, though it embarrassed the waitress, and we decided to leave her a big tip.

I couldn't get to anger. I was stuck in sad; sunk in the murky mess of it. I am a firm believer in tears and I'm a great crier, but the ground around me was saturated with my grief and I wished for sharp, hard anger on which to stand, with which to fight, to move me out of the muck.

We passed on dessert only because Ann had to be back at work for a meeting. On my way home, I was craving something sweet. I decided to stop at the Dairy Queen located between a pizza place smelling of baking cheese and garlic and a paper outlet store with balloons and tissues of every color displayed in the window. After studying the menu printed on the wall behind the clerk, I was certain that anything I ordered would upset my stomach. But in a moment of recklessness I asked for a chocolate malt.

In the car, at every stoplight, I sipped and scooped. I was getting cocky. By the time I pulled into our garage I was holding the steering wheel in one hand and the malt in the other. The straw in my mouth was making that strange searching sound trying to find every last drop hiding in the bottom of the cup, and I was celebrating. I had made it home unscathed. I leaned against the seat and wondered if I would be this lucky tomorrow. I'd be driving almost an hour on the freeway to Dreamfield Farms where, after many pep talks from Ann, I'd made arrangements to take my first horseback riding lesson in fifteen years. During the lesson, there would be a few small jumps for me to trot over and to make a mess of.

Going horseback riding made absolutely no sense when far simpler things like picking up laundry and meeting a friend for lunch were so terrifying. But life was short and there are certain things worth taking risks for. Chocolate malts. Horseback riding. They both fill me up and add sweetness to my life. It's worth taking risks for joy.

I entered the house with Mickey's dry cleaning over my arm, felt my stomach begin to roll, dropped the plastic wrapped suit on the kitchen counter, and rushed to the bathroom. I'd been right about that malt.

September 21, 1998 3:00 A.M.

The phone rang and Mickey grabbed it before he was fully awake. We had learned not to panic, as middle-of-the-night calls from our active daughters were not uncommon. We both assumed that this call was from Lani on her backpacking trip. She and two friends from college had given themselves graduation presents of student tickets to travel the world. It was a cheap plane ticket that they could continue to use as long as they kept going in the same direction. So Emily and Greg and

Lani had gone West. They flew from Boston to Los Angeles and then to Fiji and New Zealand. I wondered which college course had taught them how completely open and accessible the world was and given them permission to belong to it so fully. When I was twenty years old, going downtown St. Paul on the city bus was a big deal. Lani had met Emily and Greg when she began rowing for the University of Massachusetts crew team at Amherst. And though she and Emily were in great physical shape from their intense training during the past two years, I was grateful that gentle 6'5" Greg was part of the trio. Two young women traveling the world alone tested the limits of my vows to be an open-minded mother. The three would be in Australia now and meeting up with Patrick, another friend from school who was studying abroad for a year at the University of Queensland.

As Mickey adjusted the phone with one hand and reached to turn on the light with the other, the cat jumped off the bed in search of a quieter place to sleep. I smiled, thinking Lani was calling because she had remembered it was my fiftieth birthday. I assumed the late hour was because she was halfway around the world, and this was probably the one chance she had this day to get to a phone.

I heard Mickey mumble "Yes. Yes." Suddenly his entire body jerked, he grabbed my hand and thrust the phone into it, jumped out of bed, and ran down the steps to pick up the kitchen extension.

I held the receiver to my ear, and a deep male voice with a thick Aussie accent began, "Mrs. Greenberg, I'm Dr. Brown from the Hervey Bay Hospital in Queensland, Australia. I'll repeat to you what I just told your husband. You daughter, Ilana, and her friends Emily and Patrick have been in a car acci-dent. Ilana is the most seriously hurt. She has a severe closed-head injury. She is unconscious and on a respirator. Her left eye is turned inward. She is very sick. We have treated her here but she needs special care. We have just helicoptered her to the Royal Brisbane Hospital, which is down the coast from us. I will give you the direct phone number to the ICU there. Ask to speak to Dr. Eustas. But do not call for two hours. It will take that long for her to arrive and be admitted."

"Is this life-threatening?" Mickey had the courage to ask.

"Yes. Please make arrangements to get here as soon as possible."

He gave us the ICU number and hung up. My hand was shaking too hard to write down all the numbers, but Mickey got each one.

There were no dramatic hysterics, no sobbing or screaming. There were only a few tears as Mickey and I hugged each other tightly and silently began our private prayers, wordless prayers, silent howls. When words finally came, I prayed to my grandfather, and I know Mickey prayed to his father. Both men seemed to be more readily available than God, and we knew we had their full attention. These men had lived into their nineties and loved Lani dearly.

Please watch over her. Please be with her. We prayed as we showered.

Please. We prayed as we tossed T-shirts and toiletries onto the bed to pack.

Please. We prayed as we made lists of whom to contact to keep our home functioning while we were gone.

Please. As we passed each other Mickey would squeeze my hand or I would touch his shoulder, and though lights were now on throughout the house, a darkness was heavy upon us.

While Mickey organized the suitcase, I called Qantas Airlines. Somehow I got connected to a very kind ticket agent in the Sydney office.

"I can get you and your husband on a flight leaving Minneapolis at 9:00 A.M. It will arrive in Los Angeles in enough time for you to take the 1:00 P.M. Qantas flight to Sydney. From Sydney, you'll need to connect one more time for the flight to Brisbane. I will put all this information into the computer. Our business office in the States will open at 7:00 A.M. your time.

Everything will be ready to ticket. And then we can give you the cheaper U.S. price and our compassion fare. Even in an emergency, finances can be a concern. I send my prayers for your daughter with you."

I thanked her, hung up, and sat waiting in the kitchen. Beyond the orange countertops, reminders of the former owner's exuberant love of the seventies, stood our dining room table. Yesterday, we had set it for a family holiday dinner that was to be held this evening. Rosh Hashanah was beginning. The Jewish New Year. We were expecting fifteen people and I had worried about how we would arrange tables so everyone could sit together. The white table cloths, the white china plates with blue trim, and the patterned linen napkins were all in place. In the center of the table was a platter for the round challah breads that symbolize our desires for a full year. A glass bowl was ready for the sliced apples that we would dip in honey to represent a sweet year to come. My grandmother's candle sticks were waiting to be lit. Though my mother's mother had died when Lani was a toddler, I often felt her presence. I loved her broken English. "Throw me out the window, the key." I loved her rice soup, the recipe in her head, never written down, now lost forever.

Oh dear Grandma Ann, I need you. What am I going to do?

❑

Tuesday, June 24, 1969

Mickey had pneumonia on our wedding day. Sweat ran down his face when he walked down the aisle, and he tilted slightly as we said our vows. The next morning, we woke slowly. He turned to gaze longingly into my eyes. Then he moaned, threw back the covers, dashed to the bathroom, and threw up. This should have been my first clue that our marriage might not be all hearts, flowers, and happily ever after.

Mickey recovered and we left for a honeymoon in Las Vegas. We returned to our room late on the second day of our trip after a morning filled with an all-you-can-eat breakfast buffet and gambling, an afternoon filled with all-you-can-eat lunch buffet and more gambling, and a half hour by the pool baking in the sun. Mickey grabbed two handfuls of soap from the housekeeping cart parked in the hallway.

"Mickey! You can't do that!"

With a twinkle in his blue eyes, he laughed. "They don't mind. And all year, every time we take a shower, we'll remember our honeymoon." He leered at me, and I rolled my eyes and giggled.

Our room was deliciously cool and quiet. Immediately, Mickey hurried into the bathroom and turned on the shower. I melted into an armchair, flipping off my sandals. I stretched out my legs, leaned my head against the soft chair back, closed my eyes, and faded away. I didn't want to move for at least an hour. After that, a little romance, a light supper in our room, and sleep was all I wanted. The bathroom door banged open, and Mickey went to the closet, pulled a fresh shirt off a hanger, and flashed his neon grin at me, dimples and all.

"Where are you going?" I mumbled, barely awake.

"We're going out for dinner and gambling."

"I'm so tired," I moaned and didn't move.

Mickey came over and rubbed my back. "You know you bring me good luck. We'll have a great time."

"Okay," I said, but I still didn't move.

I'm sick of gambling. I don't like to gamble. It's boring and I'm tired. This is our honeymoon. Can't we just be quiet together. I thought my look said it all, but apparently Mickey didn't see it.

He sat on the edge of the bed to put on his shoes and flashed another smile. "*Come* on, honey. For me. I will find you the best steak dinner in town. Or lobster. Would you like lobster? Wait. I know what you want. A hot turkey sandwich with mashed potatoes and gravy. And if you want, we can have them skip the turkey and just fill your plate with mashed potatoes and gravy. How about it? Anything for my bride!"

"Boy, you are too good to me. It's a toss up between mashed potatoes and macaroni and cheese." I sighed and returned his smile. Being the nice girl I was taught to be, I convinced myself that I didn't really mind his plans, and I was grateful my love of starch hadn't caused me to blossom into triple-digit dress sizes. I wondered how Mickey couldn't tell that I didn't want to go out. It never occurred to me that even if he could tell, it wouldn't matter.

Half an hour later as the elevator purred down to the lobby, a debate raged deep in my subconscious.

Why didn't I just say how I felt?

You know what happens when you do that.

I have to speak up if I'm going to survive this marriage.

If you speak up, Mickey won't like you any more.

I need my voice.

What you need doesn't matter.

Please, I want to speak.

Why? Your opinions are worthless.

I didn't hear the exact words, though I felt the whispers, the sadness, and isolation. But I was on my honeymoon and I was supposed to be happy. I forced a smile as I reached up to straighten my hair, watching Mickey count the casino chips he pulled out of his pocket. The elevator doors opened to casino clatter, flashing lights of slot machines, and artificial laughter of people trying too hard to have fun. For years afterward, I dreamed of being trapped alone in an elevator as it flew down the shaft or spun sideways through a building like a terrifying amusement park ride. Dreams from which I woke dizzy, nauseated, and alone.

Fifteen years slipped by before I found my voice. But I had no idea what to say until after my daughter's accident.

❏

September 21, 1998 5:00 A.M.

Two hours finally passed. We called the Royal Brisbane Hospital and the number connected us directly to Dr. Eustas in the ICU. He confirmed the seriousness of Lani's condition. Severe closed-head injury. Two fractures in her skull. Unconscious. Respirator. Collapsed lung. Complicated break of left arm.

"She is very sick. You need to get here as soon as possible. She is very sick."

We gave him our estimated arrival time. As the doctor spoke, I began to curl up on myself. By the time the conversation was over, I was lying on the floor shaking violently while our cat stood guard, green eyes wide, watching for the danger. The doctor assumed that Lani had been thrown from the car. I pictured her lying alone in the grass and I ached.

By 6:00 A.M. we were packed, showered, and ready to go. We began the phone calls. The first call was to our older daughter, Shira, who was now living in Albuquerque. She knew something was wrong immediately. "What's wrong, what happened, what's wrong, tell me, tell me, tell me what it is, what happened, what? I'm coming with you. I'm coming with you. I have to come with you."

"Yes. We will make flight arrangements for you. Do you have a valid passport?"

"No, it's expired."

"We'll make sure you get an emergency one."

Do we have valid passports? Where are they? Oh, God.

The next call was to my parents. I choked, holding back my tears and their voices cracked, but they stayed calm. Twenty-two years ago this month my father had been in a near-fatal crash of a small plane. I'm sure the horror of that experience immediately flashed through their minds. When Lani was born, my father was still in the hospital recovering. We gave Lani the Hebrew middle name of Chaia, meaning Life, in gratitude for my father's survival. Ilana in Hebrew means tree.

A tree of life. May it be so.

My parents offered to call my brother, Louie, who lived in Boston with his wife Terry. And my mother also took over the job of calling and canceling all the guests we were expecting for dinner.

I called Gretchen, our neighbor and cat sitter. She agreed to take care of our house and cat indefinitely.

I called Shannon, Shira's best friend whom we considered one of our daughters. At one time, she had lived with us for almost a year to ease her financial stress. "You're going to need money. I will give you money to help with expenses." She was offering, without hesitation, what she had so little of and what she struggled so hard for. I did not accept the money, but I did accept the gesture of love.

I called Barb Herman, a business associate and dear friend. We were both marketing directors in Mary Kay Cosmetics, building our businesses and dreaming of pink Cadillacs. "I will leave my calendar for you in our front door," I said. "Cancel any appointments you don't want for yourself."

I called my friend Ann who was going to Australia next month with her husband and got her answering machine. "Will you be close to Brisbane? Do you know people we could contact?"

I put down the receiver. The phone rang. My heart stopped. This is so dangerous, picking up the phone.

"Hello, Barb. It's Louie."

My brother. My brilliant brother. I wanted to wrap my arms around him and not let go. When we were very young, he hid behind furniture and threw pick-up-sticks at me. When I was in high school, he did my math homework for me, even though he was two years younger. For my eighteenth birthday, he painted a picture for me, using the entire inside wall of a warming house at a neighborhood park. It was my best gift ever. I still meet women who, when they find out I'm Louie's sister, giggle and blush and admit to having had major crushes on him.

"The folks called, but they're not making much sense." His voice was strained. "Tell me exactly what's happened to Lani." I updated him, being as precise as possible. Lani had lived in Boston with Louie and Terry for most of the summer. My brother and my daughter had a very special relationship. He was a combination uncle, protective big brother, running partner, and workout buddy. He had been a marathon runner and even now in his forties, he could still outdistance Lani.

"I love you, Louie."

"I love you, too."

I hung up, and the phone immediately rang again.

"Hello, Mrs. Greenberg. This is Scott. We met last spring when you came to Amherst to visit Lani. Do you remember?"

"Yes, I do." How could I not? I watched how they looked at each other, how they walked with each other. They'd met when they were both rowing on the University of Massachusetts crew team. This past spring, the women's team had placed fourth in the country at the NCAA Championships in Atlanta. Lani was in the stroke seat and in the best physical condition possible. The average size for the women rowing crew was six feet and our daughter, the smallest in her boat at a mere five foot seven inches, was determined, focused, and a fighter. I needed to keep remembering that.

"Lani probably told you we were both in Boston this summer, and we spent a lot of time together before she left on her trip. I just got a call from Greg. He told me about the accident and I wanted to know if you could tell me what's happening."

I gave him the same information I gave Louie and told him to check in with my brother as often as he wanted for updates.

Mickey got on the other extension. "Scott, what did Greg have to say about the accident?"

I don't want to hear this.

"Well, as far as I know, Patrick had just joined them a few days ago. They had all been staying at this youth hostel. This morning, Emily and Patrick and Lani decided to go to a cove and swim with dolphins." Scott's words were rushing out. "Greg said that for some reason he didn't feel like going. He said he watched them pile into a car, and a driver from the youth hostel took them away for their adventure. Now Greg says he's at the police station answering questions."

Greg, what angels were watching over you?

We said our goodbyes, and Mickey took over the phone. He called his brother, Harley.

"I'll be there to take you to the airport. When does your flight leave?"

He called his older brother, Phil.

"Can you wait to call Mom until I get to her apartment? She shouldn't be alone to hear this news."

He called his administrative assistant, Dianna, and gave her a list of duties.

"When you get to the office, clear my calendar of any trials. Any weddings that are scheduled should be given to other judges to perform. Most important, begin contacting the senators' offices to arrange an emergency passport for Shira."

After he hung up, my parents called to say they'd be at the airport to see us before we left. That would be good.

By now it was 7:00 A.M., time to call Qantas Airlines again. Mickey found a credit card that he kept for emergencies and Qantas found us in their computer. Yes, they would arrange our tickets from Minneapolis to L.A., and yes, they would arrange Shira's ticket from Albuquerque to L.A. so we could all travel together for the longest part of the trip.

"You'll need visas, but don't worry. We can process them while you are on the phone. It will just take a little time."

When I finally hung up, Shira had her flight information, Harley had arrived, his car was packed, and the motor was running. He was a taller version of Mickey, complete with glasses and dimples. Both had brown hair with distinguished gray at the temples, Harley just had a little less. Since there were no words to say, he used none. He offered us his strong hug and a very considerate silence all the way to the airport. Mickey sat in the front seat and I in the back, but we managed to hold hands the entire drive. Harley backed his car out of our driveway a little after 8:00 A.M. and our flight left at 9:00. On a good day, the drive to the airport is thirty minutes. And even though we were hitting the remains of rush-hour traffic, Harley was a very conscientious driver and never let the speedometer go over fifty-five miles an hour. I thought of hollering, *"Floor this baby, NOW"* but I controlled the impulse because I was getting on that flight even if they had to call it back to the gate or I had to chase it down the runway and flag it down like it was an overgrown taxi cab. When we pulled up in front of the terminal, Harley put on the emergency brake and got out of the car. He dug into his pockets and gave us all the cash he had, then silently hugged us goodbye.

Either the terminal was quiet or I was so focused that I saw nothing but the one ticket counter without a line. Then, out of the corner of my eye, I saw friends rushing towards us. Bob, big and gruff, with a heart of gold, was waving his hand in the air. "Take this! Take this!" His voice boomed and echoed. He caught up with us and pressed a fistful of Australian currency into Mickey's hand. "This is left from a vacation we took years ago. It's your cab fare to get from the airport to the hospital. Then you won't have to deal with money exchange problems until later."

He was out of breath and so was his wife, Bobbie, who was just appearing on the scene, unable to keep pace with her husband's giant strides. Her glasses had slid down her nose during the mad dash through the airport, making her look very judicial, as if she'd been studying briefs all morning. Her courtroom was next to Mickey's on the seventeenth floor of the Government Center, and the two had become best friends, sharing lunches and consulting with equal enthusiasm over legal issues and local gossip.

We were stunned. "What are you both doing here?"

"Dianna called us," Bob answered.

Bobbie added, "She wanted help reassigning your cases, and as soon as we heard what had happened, we rushed to the airport hoping we'd find you. Now that we're here, how can we help?"

There wasn't much time and it was quickly decided that Bobbie accompany Mickey to a bank of telephones while Bob stayed with me as I checked in at the ticket counter. The plastic cheer of the clerk changed to genuine concern when she realized our situation. Even so, it took her and her supervisor too much time to find our reservations in the computer, and they called the gate to make sure the plane didn't take off without us. Finally, tickets in hand, and luggage checked through to Brisbane, we hurried to the departure gate.

Mickey had spent the past ten minutes on the phone with his ninety-two-year-old mother. He knew by the time we arrived at the airport Phil would be with her in her small apartment. Grandma, Baubie, had arrived in America from Russia when she was five years old, traveling with her family in the steerage section of an old ship. She lived through the Depression and two world wars. She raised three sons and now had seven grand-daughters, Lani being the youngest, and two great-grandchildren. Though Baubie was barely five feet tall and weighed just over ninety pounds, her frailty was an illusion. She would hold herself together, and she would hold the family together. Of this, I was certain.

Mickey and Bobbie now stood grimly next to my parents, who had been waiting anxiously at the gate for the past half hour. My folks, both in their seventies, were dressed for the synagogue, my dad in a sport coat and a dapper bow tie and my mother in a new beige suit. I don't know how they managed to dress so accurately under such stress. I wore my jeans and a sweat shirt that could have been inside out. My parents were planning on going to the Rosh Hashanah morning service, probably believing it was the best place to be. Maybe it was. Maybe their prayers would be answered more quickly. Dad stood hunched and mute, and Mom was stiffly holding back tears.

We were the last to board the plane, so our farewells were rushed. The hugs from my parents would have broken my heart if it weren't already in pieces. Dad embraced me, silently sending his love. Mom hugged me and whispered, "Be strong." They looked so lost that Bob and Bobbie instinctively stepped closer to them as Mickey grabbed my hand and we rushed into a terrifying unknown.

We stowed our carry-on items, sat down, and buckled up as the plane began to move onto the runway. Now there was nothing to keep me busy, to distract me, to keep the reality at bay.

Breathe normally, Think clearly. Be strong. Hold hands. I saw Ilana lying alone in the grass. *My Lani. Be strong, Lani.*

I remembered driving her to the airport for this trip and mumbling to myself all the way there. "It's okay. It's fine. It's okay." Lani just shook her head and punched the radio stations trying to find the new Dave Matthews song. Did my mother's instincts tell me something was terribly wrong and I didn't listen? What would I have done differently: insist she didn't go? No, I wouldn't have done that. And why didn't I know she was in trouble and wake during the night sensing something was wrong? Am I a defective mother? Must be.

As soon as we were airborne, Mickey took the portable phone from the holder on the seat in front of him to check in with Dianna for an update.

"I just heard back from the senator's office. Shira can get her passport in L.A. She should have enough time to arrive from Albuquerque, get to the federal offices, and then join you for the remaining eighteen hours of travel. And I gave all this information to Shira. You can't contact her now. She's already on her way to Los Angeles."

Mickey hung up and leaned back, bristling with frustration. As a judge, he functioned in a world where he maintained authority and control. People stood when he entered a room, followed his orders, and if they were smart, laughed at his jokes. With an early morning phone call, his illusion of control had disappeared, and a new reality was settling on him like the stale, recycled air in the plane. I understood how his stomach tightened and where the pain would settle behind his eyes. He was experiencing the place I had spent most of my life. I had arrived there at an early age, overwhelmed, trying to please everyone. I believed I was being good and didn't understand that I was slowly giving away pieces of myself in order to be loved. Now a small voice, barely a whisper, warned me that I needed to be whole again. I didn't know I had been thrust into a struggle that would lead me back to myself.

❏

February, 12, 1978

Shira and Lani were born four years apart with a miscarriage separating the pregnancies. With two children, the amount of work seemed not to double, but to triple, as if a basic principle of physics mutated when babies and children were involved. Some days were filled only with washing clothes and washing babies. Some days were taken up with the marathon event of packing up an infant and a toddler and going to the grocery store, especially in the winter. I would put a clean diaper on Lani, put her squirming body into a snow suit, and place her safely into the baby carrier. Then I would attempt to help Shira get on her jacket and boots, which, of course, she insisted on doing herself. As we were about to head out the door, Lani would make a face and there would be a soft noise and a familiar smell. I would unzip the snow suit to find a stain spreading down her leg, the diaper not the effective tool it was cracked up to be. So there was a quick wipe down, a fresh outfit, and back into the snow suit and the carrier. I imagined a crowd cheering when she was finally strapped into the car. But where was Shira? She'd taken off her jacket and was in the kitchen pouring grape juice into a glass, spilling a small river onto the floor.

By the time the girls were six and two, I was in danger of disappearing, certain I would soon wander down an aisle in Wal-Mart, never to be seen again. So I followed a survival instinct and decided to resume horseback riding.

Riding had kept me from disappearing in high school, and I hoped it would help me now. I still loved open spaces, fresh air, and the barn smells of sweet feed and leather. There was a freedom and a magic to it. Horses recognized my silent hidden parts, and with them I didn't need my voice to be understood.

But horses can be an expensive hobby. After my high school day was over, I would take the bus downtown to work at Newman's Clothing Store, and I would save all my earnings for my passion. When I wasn't working, I spent long hours riding with friends at Merrywood Farms, taking jumping lessons and even competing in a few shows. Though the barn was only a half hour from our home, the sky was always bluer, the trees greener, the air more electric. Fresh, muddy springs turned into hot, sticky summers that cooled into crisp, dry autumns and sharp, brilliant winters. These were the same seasons I experienced in the city looking out my bedroom window, but at the farm they felt clearer, truer, just as I did. I was addicted to the dust and the sweat and the highs of galloping over a course of jumps in a fluid steady pace, and the lows of failing to do anything right no matter how hard I tried. I loved it all. It made me feel strong, capable, powerful.

As soon as I began riding again, even though fifteen years had passed, I felt saved but a little confused that it was not a kiss from the handsome prince that brought me back to life.

It had always been my dream to buy my own horse. Since Mickey and I didn't have a lot of money, I bought a small three-year-old bay gelding named Tattoo. He had one white sock and a faint white spot on his nose that my trainer called his panic button. She said she didn't know who panicked more during lessons, Tattoo or me. Still a baby at age three, he had no brakes or steering, so my first job was to teach him to stop and to turn. As he matured, he learned to respond to the subtle squeeze of my legs on his sides or the gentle pressure of my fingers closing around the reins. He loved to jump, and he showed me his huge heart.

He taught me discipline, persistence, courage—all those things that we learn when we pursue the best that seems just beyond our grasp. And there was always something new to learn, if I paid attention. Always another level of grace, power, and beauty to develop. Always another challenge. If I got too comfortable with our accomplishments, Tattoo woke me with a swift buck that sent me flying into the dirt.

Ah, yes! Horses, like life, have beauty, grace, and power, but they also have the ability to dump me on my ass when I least expect it. But, with horses as with life, that's no reason not to get on for the ride.

I went to the barn three or four mornings a week, always with a supply of carrots that Tattoo would look for as soon as I opened his stall door, like a two-year-old searching for cookies. I would lead him to an empty paddock where he could run loose, where I hoped he would let out any bucks of which I would otherwise be the recipient once I got on to ride. When he stepped into the fenced ring, I could almost hear him say, "Watch what I can do, Mom." He snorted and was off, running and jumping and shaking his head. If there were a mare nearby, he would squeal to make sure he got her attention and she could see what a truly magnificent animal he knew he was. Then he'd race back to me and make sure I was still there, twirl around on his hind legs and take off again. After his morning romp, I rubbed him down before putting on the saddle. He held my grooming brush in his mouth until I was ready to use it. When I bent over to pick out his feet, he would bend his neck down and wiggle his soft nose against my back, "Watcha doing down there, lady?"

After two years of training, of aching legs and an aching back, (mine, not Tattoo's); after lessons in the middle of the winter, not being able to feel my toes, and lessons in the middle of the summer, dripping with sweat before I even got on to ride; after tears of frustration that I will never be able to do this, and tears of relief that there was still hope for me, we began horse showing.

In July, I came home from my best show yet. "Mickey, you won't believe it. We jumped the highest round of fences we've ever done. Three-and-a-half feet. Considering that we started at two-and-a-half feet last summer, I can't believe we did it. It doesn't sound very high, but when you're galloping down to those jumps, they look like mountains."

I was so excited, I couldn't stop rambling. "And Tattoo was so good. What a trouper. He trucked right around that ring and didn't bat an eye. In fact, I think he liked jumping the higher fences. And you should have seen him when I gave him a bath at the end of the day. He shook just like a puppy and then went into the pasture and found the perfect place to roll in the mud, scratching his back and his four legs kicking in the air."

I didn't notice that I was talking to myself. I thought I was sharing my good fortune with my best friend. "My trainer said we held our own, competing against horses that were fancier and had cost their owner's two or three times as much. She was really proud of me and said it was clear all our hard work was paying off."

"Can you not talk about that now, I'm watching TV. Besides you know how boring I think all that stuff is."

He landed a direct hit without laying a hand on me, and since there were no physical bruises, I didn't think I was in danger. I left the room before he could do it again. I was too tired to fight back. All I wanted was a shower. Pulling off my boots, I thought about the hundreds of nights I sat home alone while the girls slept and Mickey was out at some "important" judicial function. I thought about all the tedious dinners I'd sat through with him and his friends as they talked about court orders and legal strategies. Talk about boring!

At the end of August, Mickey took me aside after dinner, as soon as the girls left to ride their bikes to the park. I was wiping my hands on the dishtowel as he guided me into the living room and sat me on the sofa. Then, with a take-charge position, arms crossed, feet apart he focused on me.

Uh-oh, what's going on? Pay attention. Stay alert. Trouble is coming.

"Barb, we need to discuss selling Tattoo."

"What?"

"We need to sell Tattoo."

"What are you talking about?" I was frozen to the sofa.

"It's strictly for financial reasons. This hobby of yours is just too expensive, and we can't afford it anymore."

"How dare you make this decision? If it's finances you're worried about, that's something to discuss as a couple. An ultimatum from you is not in order. I'll get a job and support my riding myself. You can't take this away from me. I won't let you."

I couldn't even look at him as I got off the sofa gripping my dishtowel. I needed to be alone, and there was no private place in the house, so I went outside to the big oak tree in the back yard. I sat in the grass, leaned against the trunk and wiped my eyes. What was going on? I didn't believe money was the issue. Was it jealousy? I could believe that. I was happy doing something I loved. Was it control? I could believe that. I was in a world that was not accessible to him, and in that world, I was successful and strong. Was he trying to destroy me? I couldn't believe that. But this was a dangerous time. I needed to stay alert, to think clearly, and to act quickly.

The next morning, I wanted to do some serious whining. I knew no nine-to-five job would allow me enough time to be with my girls, let alone time to train and ride competitively. I needed some advice, so I made a lunch date with Diane, a friend from the horse world who had her own business.

At the restaurant, Diane and I slipped into a booth by the windows, gave our food orders to a brusque waitress, and I poured out my woes. Diane listened carefully, her blond hair pulled back in a tight bun, a no-nonsense person who fiercely protected her friends and those she loved. When our food arrived, she picked up her napkin and looked at me. "You need your own business. I think you should sell Mary Kay Cosmetics. I'm told it's an excellent company."

"Whaaa…?" Eyes wide, fork halted between my salad and my open mouth, I stared at her. Then I began to giggle. "Cosmetics?"

"Cosmetics," she nodded decisively. "You can sell cosmetics. Set your own hours and you can still have time to be a mom and ride."

I had the sense that this was not a suggestion. She had already made up her mind, and I'd better be smart enough to follow her advice.

Wearing no makeup, dirty jeans, and boots, I sat and had the best laugh I'd had in years and had to cover my mouth, not wanting stares from the other diners. Diane watched me, nodded, picked up her fork, and began to eat. With one more small chuckle, I turned my head to look out the window and thought, 'I am desperate, and desperate times call for desperate measures.'

The next week, Diane introduced me to a Mary Kay marketing director. Out of all the information she gave me about the company, the only fact I remembered was that any products I purchased to use for inventory had a ninety-percent buy-back guarantee in the first year. Since I couldn't imagine this career lasting longer than six months, that policy was an important consideration.

My first appointment was with Ellen who agreed to listen to my presentation so I could practice. We had been friends since before grade school. At our high school reunion, she recommended that we stand against the wall so everyone would remember who we were. The yellow concealer I gave her to use under her eyes made her look jaundiced. The lipstick I chose did not improve matters. As soon as the appointment was over, I thanked her, threw my samples into my tote, and hurried out of the house for a quick getaway. As I walked down the front sidewalk to my car, I heard a pleading voice behind me, "Please, Barb, is there any way I can purchase any of your products?" It appeared I had begun my new business.

Mary Kay is committed to empowering women and encourages local weekly meetings to motivate as well as train their sales force. I attended my meetings conscientiously and received excellent business training, but the motivational cheerleading made me want to run from the room. "You can do it." "Reach for your dream." "What you believe, you can achieve." It was assault by sound bites. An assault that would only give me a flesh wound, but if not treated quickly, I'd become so cheerful, I'd really piss someone off.

But I met successful women in the business whom I respected, who encouraged and supported me unconditionally, even though they made no commissions from my work. They didn't care how many mistakes I made, and they understood my fears. Their faith in me was powerful. I began to believe I could do "It," although I wasn't quite sure what "It" was. I could reach for my dreams, whatever they may be, and possibly, I could achieve...something. I assumed that I was entering a shallow world of lip gloss, blue eye shadow, and big, blond, Texas hair. Instead, I was being nurtured, and I was finding strength.

And Diane was right. Soon, I was covering my horse expenses and I still had time to ride and be a mom. Sometimes Lani came with me to the barn, but Shira had found another passion: dance.

She had always loved to dance in front of her bedroom mirror, her long brown hair in ringlets around her face, and her blue eyes bright from the magic of her imagination. When she was five, we took her to see a dance performance of the *Nutcracker*. When the lights dimmed and the orchestra began, she stood next to her aisle seat and closed her eyes and danced to her private visions of sugar plums. Five years later, she was on stage, dancing in the same production. In her twenties, she took her passion for dance to Albuquerque and began a company that provided dance to all children, regardless of their situational barriers, be they financial or physical. Students could take classes on scholarship and could take classes in wheelchairs. Shira wanted no child to miss the miracle of dance.

Lani was the rider. When she was ten years old, she began taking lessons on Gertie, a sweet brown mare. Whichever way Lani would tip, Gertie would manage to stay underneath her. When Gertie was put up for sale, Mickey agreed to purchase her as long as I was responsible for all the monthly bills, the board, the vet, the shoes, the lessons, all of it. I accepted his offer instantly, and on a cold February afternoon, we drove Lani to the barn for her weekly lesson. On Gertie's stall, tacked on the wooden door, was a big red ribbon and white poster board with a poem written on it:

Roses are red, violets are blue,

I'm so happy, because now I belong to you!

Unsure, Lani opened the stall door and found Gertie with a red ribbon in her forelock. The hug she gave me made it clear that I had made the right decision. But after a few months, it was also clear that I couldn't afford to support two horses. And I had to make another decision. I didn't want Lani to ride because it was important to me, but I also didn't want her to miss out on the experience if it were something she truly wanted. Believing that I'd had my turn and that now it was Lani's, I sold Tattoo; the horse I had owned for six years, whom I had trained and loved, the horse that rescued me and taught me so much. I sold Tattoo to a teenage girl who lived out of town. I wasn't at the barn when she came with her horse trailer to take him to her farm in Southern Minnesota. I sold Tattoo and never saw him again. Mickey never said a word. Not "I'm sorry," not "It's too bad it turned out this way," not a hug or a word of sympathy. I grieved alone and I grieved hard.

❑

September 21, 1998, 11:30 A.M. Los Angeles

The plane landed in Los Angeles. Mickey and I ran from the Northwest terminal to the Qantas terminal where the mob of humanity seemed to have as much forward motion as a pot of stew. Doing our best to avoid the very young and the elderly, we plowed our way to the ticket counter.

"Oh, excuse me." I shoved between a starry eyed couple in their twenties.

"Pardon me," Mickey elbowed passed a woman with a briefcase.

"So sorry." I slammed into a man wearing a baseball cap.

A Qantas security assistant spotted us as we approached the ticket counter, probably noticing passengers flying out of our path. "You must be the Greenbergs. Your daughter, Shira, has already arrived and is on her way to the passport office. It's close to the airport and she has plenty of time to make it back for your flight."

"How is she doing?" I wanted one child to be safe.

The uniformed assistant, a lovely woman with thick dark hair paused, and said tactfully, "I think I calmed her down a little."

Oh, dear Shira.

"This must be very difficult for you. If you'd like, you can use our office to make phone calls and have some privacy. Just go around that corner at the end of the ticket counter, and it will be the first door on your left. I'll stay here and watch for your daughter."

"Thank you." I almost hugged her before we rushed away. The office was a large room, brightly lit and filled with a maze of desks loaded with computers and ringing telephones. The employees scurrying by scarcely glanced at us as we rushed to an empty counter along the far wall and sat down by a quiet phone. For a moment, we paused and stared down at this instrument, as if it were the phone itself we feared, this miracle tool that brought voices with beautiful accents and terrible messages into our home, into our lives. Then Mickey picked it up and dialed, and I leaned close to listen.

"Yes, this is Dr. Eustas. She's stable. Please hurry. When will you be here? Please hurry." I wanted stable to mean good, but I knew it meant only no change.

Mickey stayed in the office to call family and I went back to the ticketing area to watch for Shira. She didn't come. Mickey joined me and we were told it was time to go to our gate. She didn't come. We waited at the gate as long as possible, expecting every person who turned the corner at the end of the hallway to be Shira. She didn't come. The final boarding announcement for our flight was called. The gate area was empty. The Qantas representative gently approached us. "It's time. I'll watch for your daughter. Don't worry. I'll get her on the next flight out. Now hurry and get on your plane."

We rushed down the jetway.

Oh my God! The plane's door was closed. Through its small window we saw flight attendants locking and securing the only path to our child. *See us, please!* A blond head turned away and then turned back and a pair of blue eyes looked out. The door was reopened and we were escorted aboard as if we were invalids, and feeling fragile, I appreciated the gesture. At first I was disoriented by the size of the plane. Instead of one aisle, there were two, and between them were additional rows of four seats each. A huge plane to carry us a great distance. We were gently led to one of those empty middle rows near the back of the plane, where we would spend the next fifteen hours with no way to contact the world.

Where is Shira? She's alone in L.A. Is she safe? I can't assume that any more. Whatever happens, I have to handle it. I'm nice. I think I'm kind. I try not to gossip much. I recycle. Why is this happening to my family? Are the rules changing? Or aren't there any rules?

Mickey and I sank deep inside ourselves. I closed my eyes and talked to Lani. "Dear Lani, if you need to leave now, I will release you with all my love and blessings. But if you decide to stay and fight, I will fight beside you with all my strength."

"I'm staying." The message was clear.

I was startled. *Am I just imagining this to comfort myself, or is this real?*

The message came again, powerfully pushing me deep into my seat. "It's real. I'm staying."

As I was trying to decide how to tell Mickey, he took my hand, leaned his head close to mine and whispered, "Lani told me she was going to make it through this."

I agreed and shared my own experience. He stared at me, shocked. Mentally and emotionally I stumbled backwards three steps.

What's wrong? What did I do wrong?

"How could you say that, about releasing her, letting her go? That took so much courage." He squeezed my hand and kissed me.

Courage? Is he crazy? I'm terrified! I closed my eyes so I could be near my daughter, wrap my mind around her. She was always stubborn so if she'd said she was staying and fighting, I knew it would be some fight. I prayed she could hear me as silently I told her, *Lani, I love you. I believe in you. You are wonderful. You are strong.* I turned to my grandfather. *Please watch over her, stay with her, comfort her. I cried to God. Please bless and protect my daughter.*

Every night for years, as I lay down to sleep, I offered that prayer for my two grown girls who were out in the world doing daring and wonderful things. I remembered the time Lani was jumping her horse in a very intense competition. We had sold Gertie to another young beginning rider and had bought Ellie, a big powerful gray mare. As they galloped onto the jumping course, something startled Ellie and she stopped abruptly in front of the first obstacle. Lani fell and injured her wrist badly. She didn't cry. She didn't whine. She went to the barn, wrapped her wrist tightly in a horse bandage, went back into the show ring, and was champion by the end of the day.

In tenth grade, Lani decided she'd compete in the prestigious show circuit in Florida when she turned eighteen. Everyone just nodded and, in effect, patted her on the head with, "Sure, sure, honey, whatever you say."

She turned sixteen on a Monday, got her driver's license on Tuesday, and got a part-time job to fund her dream on Wednesday. Every morning before school, no matter what the weather, she went to the barn and trained. And after school, she went to her job, working in the child care facility of a health club, watching little ones while their moms worked out. By December of her senior year, she'd finished her course work a semester early. On January 3rd, she packed her suitcase and her car, left for Florida with her trainer and four horses, and competed successfully on the winter show circuit for three months. When she makes up her mind, nothing dares to get in her way. If anyone is a fighter, it's our daughter.

Shira, too, fought for her dream. With critics saying it couldn't be done, she created a dance company in Albuquerque that was making a difference in children's lives. She had also left home early, blazing a trail for her younger sister. Before she settled in Albuquerque, she often took to the open road in a trusty silver-gray 1982 Chrysler she'd named Maurice. In 1990, when she was seventeen, Shira left on her first extended road trip, driving from Minneapolis to California. The morning of her departure, Maurice was in the driveway with his motor running, and Shira was in the driver's seat. I gave her one last kiss goodbye through the open car window. She smiled up at me, sunglasses sliding down her nose, her grand curls alive with expectations of dancing in the wind that would soon be blowing through them.

"Mom, I have a quick question. How do I get to the highway?"

I almost fell over. "You're going to California and you don't know how to get out of town?"

She grinned. I gave her directions. She put Maurice in gear, waved goodbye, and shouted through the window as she pulled away, "I can't believe you're letting me do this."

I laughed. How wonderful to have the confidence to put your car in gear, not knowing where the highway is, but certain you will find it. Both my girls had the ability to do that, to trust the open road and the journey.

I closed my eyes and saw the faces of my daughters, snapshots of them that I carried in my mind and thought of how they pursued their dreams. When skeptics said it could not be done, they did it. They saw the endless possibilities of life and trusted their vision, which I had never done for myself and wondered now if ever I could.

Now possibilities unknown, trust or not, I opened my eyes and found a passenger standing in the aisle next to my seat. He leaned down and asked if he could move to the empty seat at the end of our row. He had a problem sitting where he was. He couldn't see the movie screen. Some problem.

Automatically I smile and nodded. *The nice girl.*

As he sat, I immediately regretted giving up our privacy and the extra room to lie down. Being nice isn't necessarily good and can be such a bad habit. Another man stood in the aisle three rows behind us talking to anyone who walked by, and some who didn't. He was a narrow, sallow man, possibly bored and lonely, but certainly loud and opinionated. Luckily, he was too busy with other passengers to notice me on my many trips past him to the lavatory. He was still going strong after forty-five minutes when Mickey and I looked at each other, rolled our eyes, and smiled for the first time since 3:00 A.M. A gift from the obnoxious angel in the aisle.

During the flight, the crew showed three movies that I couldn't watch, and served three meals that I couldn't eat. I did manage to sleep for half an hour late in the flight. Mickey ate and slept. How did he do that? I was torn between disgust at his insensitivity, and jealousy at my inability to do the same thing. We rarely reacted the same in any situation, and before we had a year of counseling this caused terrible tensions. After our sessions we'd laugh about how different we were, but looking back I see that beneath the laughter nothing much had changed. Mickey still believed any reaction or response different from his was wrong, while I did my best to reassure myself that it wasn't so, and vigilantly limited the number of sentences I began with "I'm sorry."

❏

November 21, 1986

I focused on my Mary Kay business to avoid the pain of losing Tattoo and to guarantee that Lani's riding wouldn't depend on Mickey's income or attitude. I didn't trust him anymore, and I didn't know if I could ever forgive him. Then one morning, out of the blue, he suggested that we go for counseling. I was impressed and grateful, until I realized he assumed he was taking me in to be fixed like a major household appliance, a backed-up garbage disposal, a leaking dishwasher, a washing machine that had lost its rinse cycle. Our weekly sessions continued regularly for six months, until spring arrived and our appointments began to focus on him. Suddenly, he decided his schedule was too full to continue therapy, an avoidance pattern I'm certain is familiar to therapists.

I shed my tears and the day I had no tears left, I invited Mickey to join me outside on the front steps. The girls were getting ready for bed, and I wanted us to have some privacy. The neighborhood cooperated. There were no sweating joggers, no children on bikes, and no families walking dogs or pushing baby strollers. The street stayed quiet and our conversation was not interrupted. "If you can't be a partner in this marriage, you'll have to leave," I said calmly.

Startled, Mickey reacted neatly by putting it back in my lap. "Tell me what to do and I'll do it."

"So you can get mad at me for telling you what to do? No. That's not how this is going to work. We need to go back to counseling *together*."

And we did.

We continued our sessions once a week sitting on the familiar green sofa, sharing a box of tissues while our therapist sat across from us nodding.

"I've always felt it was my responsibility, my job, to avoid fights and keep the peace," I confessed.

Nodding, "And how does that make you feel?"

"Resentful."

Nodding, "And how does that *physically* make you feel?

"I get terrible headaches."

With a nod, she leaned forward slowly. "You don't have to do that any more. Your responsibility is to speak your truth. That may sound profound, but it only means to say how you feel. That's how you begin to honor yourself."

My eyes filled with tears.

"You've never been allowed to do that. And it's time."

I sniffled.

She nodded.

Mickey sniffled, too. And nodded. And sighed. He vowed to stay open and not close down emotionally. Of course, he respected me. Of course, he was honest with me in all areas of our life together. Of course, he would never lie to me or do anything as deceitful as have an affair.

Of course, I believed him.

I worked hard to use my voice and speak my mind, even if I had to fortify myself with a few chocolate chip cookies first. "This makes me feel sad." *Munch.* "That made me angry." *Munch.*

I bought nice new spiral notebooks and began journaling. I discovered buried rage, years of repressed anger, screams never released, frustration never admitted. I wrote viciously, filling my notebooks and throwing them away, too dark and mean for anyone to see. Beneath the rage was fear. A little girl lying in the dark, curled in her bed, hiding under layers of blankets, hearing menacing voices whisper. *It's not safe out there. Hide yourself. Be perfect. Don't make mistakes. Avoid conflict at any cost or people will notice you.*

This child tries her best to obey the voices. Everyday, she gets up and manufactures the Barbara the world will see, the Barbara who tries so hard to be clever and bright and, of course, so very nice, always nice, and she is exhausted. But light is coming into the dark room, and light always helps. Soon the elevator dreams are no more.

❏

September 21, 1998, 10:00 P.M. Australia

We stepped off the plane in Sydney and were handed a message saying Shira was on the next flight. She would arrive at the hospital at about 9:00 A.M. One daughter is safe.

Later, Shira told us that she'd had plenty of time to get back to the airport. Her cab driver was compassionate and fast and broke a few traffic rules in the interest of speed. When he slammed on his brakes in front of the passport office, he insisted on waiting for her so he could rush her back for her plane. Once inside the office, a little bureaucrat with a little power refused to put his little stamp of authorization on her passport until he proved he was in control. She tried every form of persuasion she could think of and then in desperation she decided simply to have a sobbing, screaming come-apart that embarrassed him into action. She ran out of the office, leaped into the cab, and as it raced back to the airport, the cabbie checked his watch, they both looked out their windows and up into the sky and saw our plane taking off. Shira had missed our flight by ten minutes.

Once back at the Qantas terminal, Shira called a friend who lived in Fullerton, sixty miles away. Without hesitation, he came to the airport to sit with her, and stood by her side when she called the hospital for an update. "Your sister is on life support and in a coma." *Life support* and *coma* are more frightening words than *respirator* and *unconscious*. Shira collapsed into the phone. Her friend held her, rocked her slowly, rubbed her back, made her eat, and insisted that she have a beer. He prayed with her for Lani's complete recovery and stayed with her the nine hours until her flight left.

As soon as we were notified that Shira was en route, and we knew there was time before our flight to Brisbane, Mickey and I focused on finding a telephone and contacting the hospital, a seemingly simple task. We found the Qantas lounge where we could have a little privacy, then walked down a flight of steps and found the phones. We thought we had the correct change but couldn't get a dial tone. It was at night and there was no one to ask for help, so we went back upstairs to find a receptionist. She didn't understand why these distracted Americans were having so much trouble, but she placed our call and we once again heard the urgent voice of Dr. Eustas.

"When will you be here? Please get here as soon as possible. Your daughter is very sick."

We're moving as fast as we can. What else can we do? We're getting closer, but we're still too far away.

I was famished. Mickey got a sandwich for me at a coffee shop, but I still couldn't eat. We went to the gate where I sat curled in a chair while Mickey paced. Finally, we boarded for the last part of our trip, and I sat looking out the window of the plane into the darkness, the unseen, the unknown.

It was after midnight when we arrived in Brisbane. We grabbed our luggage and, because of the hour, got through customs immediately. We found a cab and gave our destination.

The driver was a large, talkative man. "The Royal Brisbane. The largest hospital in the Southern Hemisphere. Which ward do you need? I want to drop you at the right part of the hospital."

"Ward 4B," I said.

"Okay, no worries. I'll get you there."

Mickey and I sat silently during the half hour-drive, while our cabbie played tour guide. "Lovely city, so much to see. This is the Brisbane River. We are passing some great restaurants over there on the right. Wonderful seafood and steaks."

At the hospital, we pulled up to an entrance. I slid over the seat, ready to get out. "No, no. This is the wrong section," the driver said. I slid back. We drove a little farther, stopped again. I leaned forward ready to jump out.

"No, this isn't right either." He looked at me with concern. "Sorry." An orderly standing outside pointed us in the right direction with his cigarette. We pulled over a third time in what seemed to be an alley at the back section of the building. I took a deep breath. This was it. The driver showed us an elevator next to a Coke machine. "Go up one floor, turn right, and the ward will be on your left." Mickey paid the driver with Bob's Australian currency, and included a tip, but the driver gave him back $3 AU, insisting it was too much.

We took our suitcases up the elevator, down the hall, turned left, and faced two narrow swinging doors.

Neurology Ward 4B/ICU.

Please ring bell and wait to be admitted.

Bell? Where is the bell? I can't find the bell. It was on the wall behind us.

The door opened and Dr. Eustas introduced himself. We dropped our luggage.

CHAPTER
Two

September 22, 1998, 3:00 A.M.

The ICU was small, and the lights were dimmed for the night. Lani's bed was the second from the door on the right.

As I went to her, my knees buckled. I didn't think anyone noticed, but two nurses grabbed me, got a stool, and insisted I sit. I remembered my dad's plane accident. His face had been shattered and was unrecognizable, so I had to look for other familiar parts of him. His hands were what I saw first. Now, I searched for something of my daughter that I could recognize. I looked at the fingers of her left hand. They were easy to see because her forearm was raised straight up from the bed, held up by pulleys, and wrapped in what looked like a temporary cast. The cast stopped in the palm of her hand so I could see her fingers. Lani's fingers.

Lani's hair. I saw her beautiful hair, thick waves of rich brown highlighted by the sun and brushed out behind her head on the pillow. But near her forehead a three-inch-square section of hair was shaved off and a shunt was buried in that bald space, secured with gauze and tape, looking like something from an old horror movie.

Lani's face. Almost. Not quite. There weren't cuts or bruises, but it was unnaturally swollen, especially her closed eyes, eyes that her closed lids could not stretch enough to fully cover.

There was a brace around her neck and the tubes in her mouth disappeared down her throat carrying breaths of air into her lungs. I watched her chest rising and falling in response to the respirator. The movement was calm and steady, reminding me of when she was a child and I checked on her at night before I went to sleep, peeking into her room, watching her breathe deeply, peacefully, dreaming her dreams.

Heart monitors were attached to her, and tubes had been inserted through incisions into each side of her chest to aid her damaged lungs. There was an IV in her arm, a pulse monitor on her finger, and a catheter.

There were blue plastic wraps on each of her legs for circulation and coils of wires on the floor. A monitor stood near her bed, next to the respirator. It had five lines of information and numbers, each line a different color, periodically beeping to ensure proper attention. The two nurses who had steadied me were working with her.

Dr. Eustas began to speak, and we shifted our attention to him. With sandy hair and slight build, looking about sixteen years old, he explained the purpose of the frightening-looking shunt. "The biggest danger she faces at the moment is the pressure on her brain. There is very little space between the brain tissue and the protective skull and with a closed-head injury, there's nowhere for the swelling and the blood to go; the pressure can build. The shunt monitors that pressure. It's recorded there, on the bottom line of the monitor, as the ICP, intracranial pressure. When the pressure gets too high, the nurses can turn a knob on the shunt and drain fluid out of her head. Then, as the pressure lessens, we can watch the numbers on the monitor drop."

Left unsaid, but very clear, was that if they couldn't control the pressure, they couldn't save her. Or, if they did manage to save her, the damage to her brain would be extensive.

Asking if we wanted to see Lani's x-rays, Dr. Eustas led us to the back of the ICU, doing his best to share any encouraging information. "Her heart is strong. No other internal organs are damaged. There is no spinal cord damage. Her top left rib is broken, and as a result, her left shoulder is swollen. The rib could have severed a major blood line, but it didn't, and it will heal on its own. Also, just before you arrived, I discovered that her right lung was filling with blood from a small tear. I had to make an incision under her right arm and insert a tube immediately to drain it. Both of her legs jerked up in response to the pain from the procedure. This is a good sign because it indicates that her brain, at least in part, is still functioning."

The x-rays showed the two breaks in her skull. One was at the back of her head, near her neck, and one in the middle of her head. We saw the damage to both lungs, the one that was bleeding and the other that was collapsed and leaking air. The x-ray of her arm wasn't there.

We returned to her bed, and Dr. Eustas remembered another piece of information. "I forgot to mention a small cut on her leg that needed stitches." He lifted her gown so we could see the cut, but what we stared at were her legs. They were bruised black. Not black and blue. Black. Solid black.

The doctor excused himself for a minute. I watched him walk out the door. He seemed too young for such a hard job. When he returned, he smelled of cigarette smoke.

While Dr. Eustas was out of the ICU, Mickey and I realized we were not retaining any of the medical information he shared. The image of our daughter filled our minds, and there was no room left for much else. Lani's nurses, Janelle and Amanda, recognized our symptoms and were wonderful about repeating everything for us, patiently and often.

We listened as they talked quietly to Lani, using her name often, explaining everything they did. Amanda smiled, "We believe that even though our patients are unconscious, at some level they hear and absorb what is going on around them."

"Lani, we're going to open your eyes and shine the torch in them." Janelle added, "Torch is Australian for flashlight, Lani. We are opening the right eye now. Good girl. Now the left eye. Good."

Amanda explained, "The light is to test if her pupils are reacting. They both seem fine, though the left eye is a little sluggish." I saw her eyes. They were empty eyes. Dead eyes.

"The monitor will beep often," Amanda continued. "Don't let the noise upset you. It doesn't signify that there's anything to worry about."

I looked again at the machine. It was tracking vital information about my daughter in a language I could not understand. Amanda repeated what Dr. Eustas had just said. "The number that needs to be watched most carefully is on the last line of the monitor. Can you see where it reads ICP?"

Mickey and I nodded stiffly.

"We don't want the number to go above thirty. Low twenties are better, teens are best. But remember, this is only a machine, and machines can never tell all the story." She spoke gently.

"Can I get close to Lani? Can I go near her head?"

"Yes, of course." Her tone was kind.

Cautiously, careful not to touch anything, I leaned down. I saw dried blood in both her ears. I whispered, "I'm here. Daddy's here. We love you. You are wonderful. We believe in you. You are strong. I love you." I kissed her cheek, though it was hard to find a place to kiss where I wouldn't disturb any tubes. I had a strong image of a warrior child. Then I realized that she was no longer a child, but a woman. So it is. A warrior goddess.

Janelle and Amanda now watched over us as well as our daughter. Amanda had soft brown eyes, and Janelle's hair was strawberry blonde. They both monitored Lani vigilantly and gently calmed us.

"Are you hungry? Would you like toast and tea?" They were wonderful hostesses. We were not the first distraught parents they'd comforted. "How about some vegemite? Have you ever tried it? It's an Australian delicacy. You must try it. You can spread it on your toast."

When the toast arrived, I found I could finally eat. Mickey spread his toast thickly with the black grainy vegemite, took a large bite, and made a terrible face. "What is this stuff? And do I want to know?"

"It's concentrated yeast extract."

"But what does that mean?" I asked.

"I suppose it's an acquired taste," Mickey grimaced, "like White Castle hamburgers back home." My stomach growled; I love White Castles.

As we were finishing our tea, Amanda and Janelle insisted that we take care of ourselves. "This is going to be a long process. Morning rounds won't begin in the ICU until 8:00 or 8:30. Then you can get an update from the doctors and you'll be able to talk to the social worker who will help you find a place to stay. Now, we want you to get some rest." They smiled, gave us pillows and blankets, and showed us to the small waiting room.

There were a few wooden chairs lining the dull, smudged walls, and two tables covered with outdated *People* magazines. A water fountain hummed loudly, and up on the wall, a TV with no off button was showing a "Gomer Pyle, USMC" episode. Now there's a nightmare.

We pulled four chairs together, dragging them across the linoleum floor, two apiece, to lie across. Mickey unplugged the TV and we tried to sleep. I felt pain begin in my right hip, and decided it was probably from the long hours of sitting on the plane. I looked around the dim room one more time, saw a cockroach climb up a table leg, then closed my eyes around 4:30 Wednesday morning, 38 hours after Mickey had picked up the phone in the middle of the night, in the comfort of our bed, in the safety of our home, and where our lives had changed in an instant.

❑

"Albert! That's not where you pee. Albert! Let me help you. Stop acting like that! You know that's not how we do things." Albert's response was loud and nasty, but he and his dutiful nurse were better than any alarm clock. It was almost 7:00 A.M. We quickly folded our bedding and went to the ICU door. Albert was nowhere in sight. We rang the bell and were admitted immediately. This time we noticed a sign directly inside the door instructing all who entered to wash their hands at the sink to avoid spreading infection. We went straight to the sink to wash, and would be washing our hands many times a day for endless days. The room was now brightly lit, revealing the harsh medical reality that would define our lives for the foreseeable future.

The neurological ICU had ten beds, five along each long wall, with the nurses' station in the middle of the room as the command center. Lani's appearance was no less shocking in full light. Even though we were prepared, I had trouble breathing. I would never get used to the tightness in my chest, the crushing of my heart, but I would learn to handle it.

Dr. Eustas, looking like a teenager who had been up all night cramming for an exam, advised us to go to the hospital cafeteria, which would be opening momentarily, where we could sit and eat before the morning rounds began. So, as though she were merely sleeping late on a Saturday morning and we wanted to let her know we'd be out running errands and would be back soon, we bent over Lani's head, murmured a few words and kissed her cheek. Then we went off in search of breakfast, not because we were hungry, but because we were being practical.

The cafeteria was quiet. Only a few people sat scattered among the tables. The large, hair-netted woman behind the counter was smiling and helpful, not yet haggard by rushing interns and worried visitors. She handed us each a plate with a triangle of hash browns, a poached egg, and a grilled tomato, and we sat down in a square of sunshine by a window and ate in silence. After we finished, we pushed aside our dishes and began planning how to communicate with everyone at home.

We decided to call Shannon, Shira's best friend and our unofficially adopted daughter, and have her change the message on our voice mail to say that we were with our daughter, Ilana. It would direct any Mary Kay customers to Barb Herman, and if friends wanted additional information about our situation they could contact Dianna, Mickey's administrative assistant. Efficient Dianna would be our point person, and Mickey would check in with her daily. The time difference between the two opposite ends of the Earth meant that if he called Minneapolis early in the morning from Australia, he would reach her at work late in the afternoon, the day before.

Our system planned, Mickey looked at me and said, "Barb, we have to talk about the different possibilities that the future may now hold for Ilana. What if she...."

"Stop! Don't say any more." I covered my eyes.

"But, Barb, what if the doctors find...."

"Mickey," I interrupted sharply, "you can't talk about what-ifs. We both know the possibilities, but right now Lani is alive, she's a fighter, and that's all I'll focus on. If things change, then I'll change my focus, but not now. No more what ifs, okay?"

"Okay." He slumped back into his chair.

I leaned my elbows on the table, put my head in my hands, closed my eyes, and pictured our warrior goddess daughter. I vowed I'd spend all my energy watching her, loving her, talking to her, believing in her.

We returned to the ICU and, as I walked through the door, I had the sensation of a metal plate slamming down through the middle of my head. The creative right side of my brain, where the what-ifs grew, went dark, as if someone turned off the light and locked the door. *Don't go there now. It's not safe.*

While my subconscious was marking parts of my mind off limits, our social worker entered the ICU and introduced herself. I didn't want to deal with the sweet condescension and sympathy of a social worker. I didn't want someone to examine my reactions or give me a formula to handle crisis.

But Lorelle took me off guard. I liked her immediately. She was honest, straightforward, genuinely concerned, and she didn't ooze. She wore a soft, flowing skirt, a simple shirt, and artsy earrings. She led us to a small, stuffy consultation room next to the waiting room where we had unplugged the TV and slept briefly. The office was crammed with a desk, four chairs, one wheelchair, one gurney, and a stack of assorted medical charts. This private room was to become our base of operations for over a week, and it had a phone, a gift from the gods. At the end of the week, the phone was gone. We had either angered the gods or the supervising nurse.

Lorelle had been busy. She'd found hotel rooms nearby for our first two nights, and after that there was a place even closer to the hospital that had space for us. She explained that because Lani had been a passenger in the car that had crashed, Australian insurance would cover all her medical expenses here and back in the States, and we might even be reimbursed for our travel expenses.

"Let me update you quickly on the status of the other people that had been in the accident with Lani." I was embarrassed to realize that I hadn't thought of them until now. "The driver from the youth hostel is fine. Emily is in the hospital in Hervey Bay. That's about a six-hour drive up the coast. Her pelvis is broken in four places and she has a severe concussion. Her father and brother are making arrangements to fly from Boston to be with her. They should be here by the end of the week."

She pushed her thick brown hair behind her ears. "Patrick is in a third hospital in Maryborough, half an hour inland from Emily, and he'll soon be transferred here, to the Royal Brisbane. His sister will be coming from Maine to take him home the moment the doctors give their consent."

"We'll keep an eye on him until she gets here," Mickey offered.

Lorelle nodded and continued. "Patrick sustained serious lacerations and internal injuries and his ankle needs special attention because a metal rod went though it, trapping him in the wrecked car for over ninety minutes." I didn't have the strength to react to what she was telling us.

"A mother and her baby were in the other car involved in the accident. The baby is fine and I think the mother only sprained her ankle. I don't have the exact details, but I can find the newspaper report for you."

My mind was processing the information, but my heart would deal with it later. When she delivered the article days later in a manila envelope, I wouldn't look at it.

"I need to tell you about something else." She hesitated, trying to be tactful. "A rabbi came to see Lani on Tuesday evening, but because you hadn't arrived, and he didn't have your permission, he wasn't allowed into the ICU. That's hospital policy.

"That's fine," I said.

"Thank you. But the rabbi left the hospital very angry and wants to talk to you. Can we call him now?"

"Of course," Mickey said.

While Lorelle dialed the phone, I whispered to him, "How did a rabbi in Australia know about Lani?"

"Well, it's Rosh Hashanah so the synagogues are packed. I'm sure a special blessing for healing was offered and her name was mentioned and that's all it took. The word went out and some serious networking was done. Someone knew someone who knew someone."

Lorelle reached the rabbi, spoke to him briefly, and handed the phone to Mickey, and I leaned in to hear the conversation. We listened to the rabbi explain that he was very upset that he'd left his family during holiday time and was not allowed to see our daughter, repeating several times how insulted and

43

inconvenienced he felt. How could he be treated like that? Didn't the staff know he was taking time away from his family? And during such a holy time of year? He ranted, he raved, but he never asked about Lani. Mickey was very gracious, but by the time he hung up the phone I was disgusted.

It was getting close to 9:00 A.M. I knew that Shira would arrive soon. I didn't want her to walk into the ICU by herself. Probably it had worked out best that she was on a later flight. Mickey and I had time to adjust to the horror and be a little stronger for her. Sitting there in that dreary room, I was startled when a strange noise escaped from me, sharp and deep. It was a sob of exhaustion, an animal sound from a mother that can do nothing to protect her young.

"I'm just tired," I managed to choke out.

Lorelle and Mickey insisted that I lie down on the gurney to rest and that they would let me know as soon as Shira arrived. In less than five minutes, Mickey gently touched my shoulder. We rushed out of the conference room, turned the corner, and there was our older daughter, solemnly walking towards us, hunched and ragged, carrying only a small backpack. Her face was gray, and the brown curls that usually had a life of their own were matted and flattened around her head. She felt frail when I hugged her, and limp, like she would melt into a puddle, bones and muscle dissolved. There were dark circles under her puffy eyes and even though she was impatient to see Lani, she agreed to first join our meeting with the two doctors who were just leaving the ICU.

The meeting in our consultation room was brief. The doctors had nothing new to say though they each said it so differently. One read off his chart blandly, looking up when he was finished with a pale smile. The other looked directly at us with round brown eyes that spoke with compassion and concern before he even said a word.

Our minds certainly were not eased, and as soon as the doctors excused themselves, we rushed anxiously to the ICU. Shira asked that Mickey and I stay at the nurse's station and let her approach Lani alone. We stood silently as she walked over to the bed, looked down at her sister and cried quietly.

The nurses let the three of us stay in the ICU all morning, working around us, repeating medical information we needed to hear. We spent the time talking to Lani, holding her hand, rubbing her shoulder, touching her cheek. We watched the monitor as the numbers fluctuated. And we watched her chest go up and down.

The only times we were away from our daughter's bedside were when we received phone calls from family and friends. Mickey or I would take the calls at the nurse's station, so we were still in view of our daughter. We would accept these precious gifts of love and support and felt them stacking higher and higher around Lani's bed.

Some people were very practical. "We don't want you driving around Australia with the stress you are under and with all the traffic on the opposite side of the road. And we want to be sure you're eating enough. So a group of us have pooled our resources and wired you $1500. Take cabs everywhere you go, and at every restaurant, think of us." We were overwhelmed.

My brother, Louie, called. "I want to be with you and Lani. I'm flying to Australia and Lani's boyfriend, Scott, is coming with me. We'll see you Saturday." My knees buckled for the second time.

Thank you Louie, my dear, dear brother.

The ICU was closed to visitors between 1:00 P.M and 4:00 P.M, a time for patients and families to get some rest. The nurses insisted we not return until the next morning, because we'd need our strength to get through whatever was to come. We agreed and said our goodbyes to Lani. "Sweet dreams," I whispered in her ear. Then we left her in the capable hands of the nurses and doctors and the watchful spirits of her two grandfathers, and the healing energy of God and the Universe. We took our luggage, found a cab, and went to our new home.

CHAPTER
Three

The Gregory Terrace Motor Inn is a two-story building on the corner of a busy residential street and a quiet side street. We walked up six steps to a charming courtyard, where we found a small pool and a few umbrella tables with plastic chairs, all surrounded by lovely trees and blooming shrubbery. Behind the pool, through sliding glass doors, was a cozy dining room. We entered the reception area where a slender, friendly young woman with short, dark hair smiled at us from behind the desk, "G'day, I'm Wendy, and we've been expecting you." She registered us quickly and efficiently. "You look tired and hungry. Which do you need to do first, eat or sleep?"

"I think we better get some food into us before we collapse," Mickey answered.

"Well, our dining room is only open for breakfast and dinner, but I know of a great place to eat that's close by and if you want, I'll call a cab for you. And don't worry about your luggage. I'll have someone take it to your room."

"That's a deal," I agreed with Mickey.

In a few minutes, the cab had arrived. We all crawled into the back seat and, within moments, it pulled up in front of a restaurant and we all crawled out. Café Boulevard was a wonderful place and became one of our hangouts. We could order salads, sandwiches, or entrees at the counter, and there were delicious vegetarian options for Shira. We could sit at tables inside or outside under a canopy near the sidewalk. We would eat there often, and on good days, when we weren't totally exhausted, we would even walk the single mile home after lunch.

The Gregory Terrace gave us two adjoining rooms. Shira could have her privacy though she kept the door between us open, so as to not feel alone. The rooms were clean and comfortable, and it felt good to have a safe place to rest. In each room was a queen-sized bed with small night tables on each side, a dresser with a TV on it, and a small table in the corner with two chairs. There was even an electric teapot, an assortment of teas, and two cups.

Before we tried to sleep, there was another flurry of phone calls. Mickey wanted to advocate for Lani as strongly as possible in the medical conferences to come, so he called Larry, whose college-age daughter had been paralyzed from injuries in a car accident three years earlier. Mickey had always respected how aggressively Larry had protected his daughter when dealing with doctors and hospitals, and he wanted advice from someone who understood the situation and could speak from experience.

Next, he talked to Max, another friend whose daughter had been very ill. Max said he'd bargained with God to save his child. I couldn't imagine a God who needed to be bribed to be compassionate, so I didn't bargain. I begged. I hollered. Certainly someone would hear me. An angel or a great spirit.

Sometimes it's the people around us who answer our prayers. That night, Lorelle, our social worker, called and explained. "I've been talking to a friend of mine who is a barrister, a trial lawyer. He wants to help. May I give you his number?"

Mickey called this wonderful stranger who offered us the use of his office, his staff, his computer, and his fax to stay in touch with family at home. He and his wife would be going out of town in a few days, so he also offered us the use of his home and his car. He wanted to meet with us to help us through the legal maze that would develop, and he would refer us to a solicitor who was qualified to work with cases such as ours.

Calmed by the generosity of this stranger, we turned off the light and closed our eyes. Lying in a strange bed, I woke every few hours to the dark and the antiseptic smell of starched hotel linens. At 2:00 A.M., we were panicked by a persistent buzzing that turned out to be the crazed alarm on Mickey's five-dollar drug store watch. At home we would have laughed, but this night we quickly silenced it by burying it under a pile of sweatshirts in a drawer.

I got out of bed in the morning, barely rested, and noticed my hip still ached. Not such a big thing, so I ignored it, showered and dressed, and we went down to breakfast. The possibilities on the hotel breakfast menu were impressive. They served a buffet of fruits and toasts and cereals, and we could order eggs, hash browns, bacon, ham, lamb chops, and spaghetti. Though it was all very tempting, we ordered only the familiar eggs and hash browns, deciding to save the lamb chops, and spaghetti for another day. Then, we set out on our first walk to the hospital. Later, Mickey, our statistics man, declared that going to the hospital took seven minutes, but because the return trip was uphill, coming back took eight. Our walk took us by small shops and offices and an entrance to a neighborhood park.

September was springtime in Brisbane, and even in the city we saw blooming tropical flowers and trees budding with new life. The nurses had warned us about crossing streets because the traffic flowed from the opposite direction than we were used to. We took their advice and at every intersection, looking like we had a nervous disorder, our heads jerked as we looked right, left, right, left, to make sure we could cross safely. That made me wonder about which side of the hospital hallways we were supposed to walk on. Left? Right? Left? Right? My dilemma unresolved, I would constantly zigzag down the corridors, like I'd been given the wrong medication.

Walking up to the Royal Brisbane this warm sunny morning, we saw that it was a patchwork of old and new, and in a constant state of repair, rebuilding, and new construction. Our shortcut to 4B/ICU, which was in an older section, took us up a relatively steep hill through an alley, where we could enter a side door directly onto the second floor. Outside the door was a row of chairs that every morning held patients in hospital gowns and robes, sometimes barefoot, all having a smoke, visiting with each other and inhaling deeply. One morning, a man in the hallway struggled to walk on crutches, with his leg in a metal brace, pulling his IV stand. I thought it was very unfair of the therapists to insist he exercise like that until I realized he was just determined to join the gang outside for a cigarette.

This first morning, Mickey said he wanted to stop at the magazine stand at the entrance to the alley. Creative avoidance? Shira said she'd stay with him. Sensitive, thoughtful daughter. I was impatient and hurried ahead. Terrified mother.

As I climbed up the alley, my chest was so tight that I had trouble breathing, a familiar symptom of my fear, but it didn't stop me or even slow my pace. I entered the ICU and, as I would every morning, I bent down to kiss Lani's cheek. I told her quietly about our hotel and breakfast and the morning walk and the exotic flowers, and I noticed fresh blood had drained out of her ears during the night.

The doctors were beginning their rounds, so I was ushered out into the hallway where I could choose to sit on either of two hard, wooden benches that looked as uncomfortable as church pews, facing the wall of 4B/ICU, the focus of our prayers and sacraments. We spent a lot of time in that hallway looking at those walls: dingy green from the floor to eye level, then a smudged cream color. Institutional walls. Tired walls. Like the worn faces of old women who had seen too much. With no pictures to cheer or give visual relief, we watched the doorway to the ward. Doctors and nurses moved in and out efficiently. Families visited, brave, stoic, emotional, exhausted. Near one bench, there were two pay phones that we learned to use. Next to the other bench was a machine that dispensed coffee and hot chocolate, often simultaneously into the same cup.

Between the benches was the hallway that led to the waiting room where we spent our first night and the office where we conferred with doctors and sought refuge as needed. At the end of the hallway was the doorway to ward 2B, where patients were promoted after ICU. I gazed down the short hallway and prayed that day would come for Lani. Mickey and Shira came with magazines and mints and informed me that they had explored briefly and found a bank branch connected to the hospital where we could open an account to transfer funds. They knew we could be in Australia for some time.

❏

This was the morning for our meeting with Dr. D'urso, Lani's primary supervising doctor. He looked grim when he came out of the ICU, introduced himself and asked us to join him in the conference room. He was tall, slender, broad shouldered, nice looking, hard looking. He wore glasses and no smile, working on maintaining a professional distance. When he gave us Lani's prognosis, I understood why. Mickey had bought a notebook to record all the doctors' diagnoses and comments, but at this meeting, Dr. D'urso insisted on writing everything down for us. First he listed her injuries, verbally and in writing.

A closed-head injury.

Two skull fractures.

A fistula behind her left eye (a tear in an artery wall that was allowing blood to pulse into a vein and create enormous pressure in her head, specifically on the optic nerve behind her left eye).

A severe dissection of her left carotid artery (separation of the interior lining from the wall of the artery).

A mild dissection of the right carotid artery.

One punctured lung, partially collapsed, leaking air.

One damaged lung, partially filled with blood.

A severely broken left arm (monteggia fracture/dislocation).

Severe bruising on her thighs and waist.

Small laceration on her left shin.

"The next forty-eight to seventy-two hours are critical," he said. "Until the brain swelling stabilizes and drops, we can't do anything. If she survives to that point, the first surgery will be to repair the fistula and balloon off the left artery. I'll tell you what the situation is as I see it." He started another list of her prognosis.

Thirty-percent chance that she won't survive.

Thirty-percent chance that she'll survive with severe brain damage.

Thirty-percent chance she'll survive with varying degrees of brain damage.

For a moment, there was not a sound. Then Mickey asked about the recovery process. Dr. D'urso had avoided that subject, his medical training telling him there would be none. He looked up at us, answering carefully. "Patients who do survive to any kind of a functioning level often have memory loss or personality changes. This may be a long process. Plan on being here a few months." Then he stood, excused himself and left the room.

We sat silent and still. Shira was the first to move. She unfolded herself from her chair, stood, and left the room. Mickey put his head on my shoulder and cried. I couldn't breathe. I looked into my heart and watched as I dug a trench deep inside myself, the place from where I would fight for my daughter's life. I would not waiver from my mission. Neither would I repeat this diagnosis to anyone. I couldn't speak it. I couldn't hear it. I pulled it down into the trench with me like a bloodied soldier, and in fear and superstition kept it locked away from fate's attention.

❑

That afternoon, we returned to our office for another meeting, this time with the insurance people. Our social worker, Lorelle, joined us to make sure we asked all the right questions and the insurance company representatives gave us all the right information. After we were seated, she made the introductions. Mickey gave everyone his intimidating judicial stare and began. "I understand how this works. I want to be very clear that I know how this game can be played and how it should be played, so I expect truthful statements about your policies, and I will hold you to your promises."

One man shifted in his chair; the other straightened his tie and responded. "Please understand that the Australian system is not as adversarial as it is in the States. We all want to work toward what is in the best interest of the patient."

"That sounds admirable, and it may be the case. I hope it's the case. But understand that I will be vigilant in making sure your company deals fairly with my daughter."

"Let me explain," the second agent leaned forward. "Because of our country's mandatory third-party coverage, and since Lani was not the driver of the car, she is automatically covered. All her expenses in Australia and at home will be paid for as long as necessary, including any long-term care or rehabilitation, counseling for her and your family, and most likely your travel expenses to Australia, and your living expenses while you are here."

Long-term care. Dear God, What kind of a future are they expecting for my daughter? Long-term care... Stop it!

The room seemed to shrink. My legs were drawn up in front of me, my side was pressed against the desk, and my hip ached.

Between these two meetings, two more religious congregations had been heard from. Dr. Eva Popper, who worked at the hospital, was president of a progressive congregation in town. She met with us briefly to offer support and to invite us to Yom Kippur services the next week.

And a pale, young orthodox rabbi with a full beard came to the hospital dressed in a dark suit, dark hat, carrying his prayer book, asking politely, "May I stand by Lani's bed and pray for her?"

We gave our permission, and he went into the ICU and stood in the midst of tubes and wires and machines, a man of faith looking as if he'd arrived from another time in history, rocking back and forth to his private rhythm and quietly chanting ancient prayers for our daughter.

❑

That evening, Shira, Mickey, and I ate dinner in the hotel dining room. It was small, casual, and comfortable, and there was familiar recorded background music. Shira started to sing along. "I got you, babe."

Mickey and I joined her. "I got you, babe. I got you babe."

We started to laugh and our laughter became manic and then turned into sobs. Our emotions were knotted together like colorful scarves in a magician's pocket, only the tip of one yellow scarf peeking out. That's what we reached for, a little brightness, only to find it was tied to deep blue panic that was in turn tied to sharp red pain. The colors faded, we calmed ourselves, and wiped our eyes.

"I have to ask you something," Shira said. "I've heard of marriages breaking up under extreme stress. Is that going to happen to you?"

Mickey and I spoke immediately, alternating our responses. "Don't worry about us."

"You don't have to worry about us."

"We love each other."

"Very much."

"We respect each other."

"Very much."

"Remember all that counseling we had?"

"We're just fine."

"Yes, honey, we really are fine."

Shira gave a weak smile and sighed. I believed we were telling her the truth. My arms were resting on the table and I laid my head on them, the white linen table cloth my pillow. I closed my eyes. Shira may be an adult, but she's still my child. How do I protect her? How do I keep the pain away? I can't.

❑

Friday morning, the doctors said that Lani's brain activity was increasing, and that, in turn, was increasing the pressure in her head, creating a very dangerous situation. They decided to give her a heavy barbiturate to paralyze her and chemically maintain the coma until the brain swelling could go down. Friday afternoon, during our break time from the ICU, we did our best to ignore the immobilizing fear while we packed and moved to a motel closer to the hospital.

When we registered, the manager gave us two beautiful ceramic bowls left for us by Dr. Eva Popper.

"Why would she give us ceramic bowls?" I was very confused.

Mickey lifted the covers. "Dinner."

The bowls were filled with rice and chicken and fruit. She had thoughtfully prepared a beautiful Friday night dinner for us. We went up to our new room and found it was clean, but very small. There were two beds, a counter about three steps from the foot of the beds with a small refrigerator under it, a sink in it, and a microwave on it. The bathroom was also very clean, but so small that we could sit on the toilet, wash our hands in the sink and turn on the shower at the same time.

It's okay. Small is okay. I can stay here. I'm tough.

At 4:00 P.M., we returned to the hospital. The young orthodox rabbi had delivered a cardboard box for us filled with challahs, bagels and cream cheese spreads, honey cakes, and candles with candle holders; all the basics for a traditional Friday night Sabbath dinner. While Mickey went to make several phone calls, I took the box into the ICU and gave the nurses most of the food since we couldn't possibly eat it all. Then I sat by the nurse's station and ate one of the bagels, tearing off small pieces and chewing slowly and deliberately, all the while watching my girls.

Shira sat next to Lani, touching her, talking to her softly, crying. How could I believe what was happening? No parent should have to look at one child, lying lifeless in a coma, while the other cries quietly by her side. I may have looked calm, sitting there eating my bagel, but I was watching from my trench, clutching my heart.

This scene in the ICU would always stay with me. As a reminder of what? I suppose I can choose what it will remind me of...pain, faith, horror, love, fear...the options go on.

Lani was the child I almost miscarried, who cried and cried the first months of her life. And who lit up the room when she finally did smile. Stubborn, bright, who didn't like to cuddle or hug, but could hold our hands and know secret things about us. She could argue with a vengeance and always called us on our inconsistencies.

Shira, the artist, the dancer, the big sister. Shira always said her strategy was to wait until she was married and had children before telling us all the things she did that we didn't know about, assuming by then it would be too late for us to get upset. How they used to fight.

"She's looking at me. Tell her to stop looking at me."

"She's touching me. Tell her to stay on her side of the sofa."

"She won't let me play with the crayons. I can play with them if I want to. Aagghh."

The screaming. The door slamming. The tears. How quickly things change.

Shira walked over to me and asked, "Mom, how do I pray for Lani? I don't want to pray for anything that's not in her best interest. I don't want her to come back to us if she can't be herself anymore. What should I do?"

"Honey, all I can tell you is what I did on the airplane. I talked to her and asked her what she wanted. You know how stubborn she is. She won't do anything she doesn't want to anyway." I tried to make Shira smile. "So I asked, and she told me that she was going to stay and fight and I believed her."

"I like that. Thanks, Mom." She went back to Lani's bedside, held Lani's hand, and a silent conversation between two sisters began.

Shira got the same strong image that Lani would return to us. From that moment on, she believed in Lani's recovery with complete faith. Even with all the evidence in front of her of the tremendous damage her sister had sustained, Shira no longer doubted the healing to come.

She believed totally in voices and visions, and her life was an expression of those private knowings. She gave me strength. In the months following the accident, I often wondered how different my life would have been if I could have heard those golden voices and had the courage to follow them. All my life, my head was so full of "shoulds" and "have to's" and all varieties of self-criticism that even if angels were speaking to me, I don't know if I could have heard them over all the racket.

We left the hospital that evening at 9:30 P.M., walked back to the new motel, opened the door to our tiny room, and realized this couldn't be our home. At the end of the day, we needed a safe, comfortable refuge, a space where we could regain energy and heal a little. This wasn't it. This was smothering, claustrophobic, and this was no time to play at being tough; this was a time to be smart.

We called the Gregory Terrace and they once again had rooms for us. The desk clerk called a cab while Shira and I packed and took our luggage outside. While we waited for our cab, Mickey sat in the dark shadows, staring at the ground, and silently collapsing into himself.

Returning to the Gregory Terrace felt like going home. We were given adjoining rooms on the second floor, and there was a room right down the hall for Louie and Scott when they arrived the next day. We crawled into bed, to sleep, to hide, to mend frayed pieces of ourselves that were beginning to unravel. When we woke, Mickey seemed revived.

Saturday morning, Louie and Scott came straight from the airport to the hospital. I was in the conference room when a nurse came to tell me they'd arrived. I rushed into the ICU and was momentarily confused, wondering why the two doctors leaning over Lani's bed were both wearing baseball caps. Then they turned around. There were long hugs and much tear wiping and nose blowing. I know Lani looked worse than they imagined because imagining this reality was not possible. I held onto my brother, not wanting to let go, repeating, "I'm so glad you're here. I'm so glad you're here."

Louie and I looked like twins. We both wore glasses and had short, dark, curly hair that was graying slightly. I thought it made my brother look distinguished and made me look old, so mine conveniently returned to its original color every two months. But while Louie had the body of an athlete, I hadn't exercised since I had stopped horseback riding and my love of macaroni and cheese was starting to show. The frivolous concerns of another lifetime.

Louie and Scott came bearing gifts. Louie had earned a Ph.D. at MIT and is our family computer genius, so he arrived with his laptop computer and a digital camera, determined to create a website for Lani in order for correct and current information to be available for family and friends at home.

Scott came with Lani's blanket, the one her Baubie had crocheted for her as a baby gift and with which she'd been sleeping since she was an infant. Over the years, the soft pastels of blue and pink and yellow had faded but never unraveled. The weight of it, its texture, and its smell always comforted Lani, and I loved that my strong, fearless daughter chose to take it with her to college. I wished for something of my own I could hold to make me feel safe. The ICU nurses didn't mind the blanket's presence until they learned the last time it had been washed. Then they sternly said Lani would have to wait for it until she was out of their ward.

When we had to leave the ICU for the afternoon, Louie and Scott gathered their luggage and we began our walk down the alley. Before we reached the street, Scott stopped, sank down onto the curb, covered his face with his hands, and cried. I sat next to him, put my arm around his shoulder and held him until the storm passed. I couldn't do this for Lani: hold her, rock her; and it helped me to comfort this young man.

During the past week, Scott had stayed in touch with Greg, who was now waiting for us when we arrived at the hotel, where there were more hugs all around. Greg bent down for us to reach him while maintaining a forced calm, with blue eyes tired and tight at the edges. Between trips to the police station and the hospitals in Hervey Bay and Maryborough, he had collected his friends' belongings from the youth hostel and presented us with Lani's backpack. He also brought the only items of Lani's that survived the crash: pieces of two necklaces that she always wore. One was a seashell from Scott and the other was a small rune stone from Shira engraved with the symbol for travel.

Everyone was hungry, and we decided to walk to Chinatown for lunch. We walked, two by two, Greg and Scott, Louie and Shira. Mickey and I brought up the rear. Mickey took my hand and asked, "How come I never realized how strong a person you are?"

"You didn't want to know, so you never looked, never noticed. You liked thinking you were the only strong one, and I didn't need to tell you any different." I looked up into his face and smiled. Surprised, he stared at me, then kissed me, a quick, almost embarrassed kiss.

I'd always been shy, and people tend to underestimate someone who is quiet. There are many of us in the world who are powerful but camouflaged, strong but overlooked. Sometimes it is our own doing, staying hidden because being visible feels too dangerous. But I am still here. I haven't dissolved. Even though I've given so much of myself away, a piece of my core held solid.

We walked silently, hand-in-hand, until we reached the bustle of Chinatown. Shops and restaurants lined both sides of a plaza filled with sidewalk vendors and shoppers. Sounds of musicians and exotic languages floated in the air rich with smells of frying food, ripe fruits, and hot crowds. Shira went off to explore and when I lost sight of her, my heart clenched. She returned in ten minutes, and we all sat down to lunch in a small restaurant. The service was fast and our food came quickly, lots of steaming vegetables and rice. While we ate, Greg told us details of the accident that he'd gotten from Patrick who'd been conscious and alert during both the crash and the rescue.

Greg tried to balance the gravity of what he was saying with his hunger. He put down his fork as he began to speak, then picked it up and put it down again. Finally, his appetite won out, and he ate as he told his story.

"The driver of the car was an employee of the youth hostel. She was from England, fairly young, and not driving well at all. Once she pulled over to the side of the road for a smoke and Emily offered to drive instead but the girl said no, said she'd be fine and just needed her cigarette. Then she started the car and drove off again. Patrick said a bird suddenly flew out of the bushes and into their path. The girl veered sharply to avoid it, went onto the shoulder, overcorrected, shot across both lanes of traffic and into the path of the oncoming van, which hit them broadside and sent their car flying down a steep embankment. Patrick and Emily were on the impact side of the car, and Lani was in the back seat behind the driver. Patrick said he remembered blood and Emily moaning."

Greg shook his head and kept eating. "The driver of the van that hit them was a young mother with her baby and they're both fine as far as I know. I think maybe the mom has a broken ankle. She was driving an Australian Holden Commodore sedan. That's a pretty solid vehicle, and it did a lot of damage to the youth hostel's little Ford Falcon. And you know what? I heard that the hostel's driver didn't get hurt at all. Maybe some bruises. I think she didn't even need to stay in the hospital. And I think she's still working for the youth hostel. Jeez, can you believe it?"

His brow furrowed, Greg gulped water and shifted his long legs. "You know, nobody's heard from her? The driver. She hasn't contacted the hospitals or sent notes or flowers, and neither has the youth hostel. She almost killed my friends, and she seems to have disappeared, run away from it all."

He put down his fork and closed his eyes. His story complete, he took a long drink of water and focused more intently on his food. I had stopped eating at the beginning of the meal to concentrate on his every word, to devour the morsels he was putting in front of me. How must Lani have felt in those seconds? Did it happen too fast for her to register fear or pain? I hope so. I pray she didn't feel the impact or hear the screaming of tires, the ripping of metal, the sobbing of friends.

The rage I felt when he spoke about the youth hostel's driver hit me like a cold hard wave pounding out of the ocean, and like a wave, after it hit, it pulled away and was gone. She would not be my focus. Lani was the only one who was important to me. Why would I want to be distracted from healing by bitterness? I wondered if the driver was so traumatized by the accident that she was hiding in the dark, ashamed and praying for forgiveness. Or had she merely shrugged her shoulders, not understanding what the big deal was, denying any responsibility or connection to these broken people. Maybe one day I will want to, or need to, deal with her, but not now.

Keeping a lid on all my emotions was exhausting. After lunch, when the others went to explore Chinatown, I went back to the hotel to lie down alone in the cool, dim quiet. I had a whole hour before everyone piled into the room. Shira walked over to me grinning and handed me a big paper bag. "Look, Mom, presents."

She sat next to me on the bed. "I know you'll be getting tired of wearing your same jeans and T-shirts over and over, so look what I found!" From the bag she pulled an ankle-length sundress printed with large flowers in soft blues and lavenders. "It was a real bargain. Only eight dollars Australian. Try it on. I hope it fits."

I hugged her and took the dress to the bathroom, pulled off my jeans and T-shirt, leaving them in a pile on the floor, and slipped the dress over my head. I walked back out into the room and did a pirouette. "Taadaa!" I was sure my bargain dress would fall apart the first time it was washed, but as Shira intended, it lifted my spirits.

"It looks wonderful. Do you like it?"

"It's perfect!"

"I'm so glad. Now look at what I got for Lani." She unwrapped a necklace, a big blue stone hanging from a silver chain. "Isn't it pretty? I think she'll like it, don't you?"

CHAPTER

Four

September 27, 1998

The day after our excursion to Chinatown, the
Gregory Terrace offered us new living arrangements. The staff thought Shira, Mickey, and I
would feel more comfortable in the manager's
apartment just down the hall from our hotel
room. It was available for long-term guests and
rarely used by any manager. The stress of moving one more time, even just down the hall,
made it a hard decision, but it was wonderful to
have a place that felt like a home. The apartment
had a small living room with a sofa, two chairs,
and a TV; a dining room with a small, black, lac-
quered table, and a mini kitchen with a refrigerator, microwave, a few dishes, and flatware. Off
the dining room, a sliding glass door opened
onto a narrow patio. Down a short hallway
were two bedrooms and the bathroom.

Every morning, I left this refuge and went to the
hospital, committed to being a watchful, alert
sentry. In the afternoon, when the ICU closed,
practical activities began to nibble at my time. We
were all running out of clean clothes, so I packed
everyone's dirty socks, undies, pajamas, T-shirts,

and jeans into a suitcase and carried it down to the basement where there were three washing machines, two of which worked, and one industrial size dryer. Sometimes, instead of running back and forth between loads, I brought along a deck of cards and played solitaire to distract myself from dark thoughts and to discourage the housekeeping staff from asking too many questions about Lani's condition. They were kind, but I needed silence.

Since we had a kitchen now, we could get groceries, so Louie and Mickey rode the ten minutes by cab with me to a shopping mall where there was a grocery store, clothing stores, and a food court. We stopped at the food court first to avoid shopping hungry and stocking up on chocolate and chips, which in my opinion is not always a bad thing. Next, we went to a woman's clothing store where I added a blouse and a pair of shorts to my wardrobe, swollen now to five items. It seems I had packed enough underwear when we left home, and I had remembered my toothbrush and shampoo. Actual clothing somehow didn't get into my suitcase.

Buying groceries would have been fun if I hadn't been so exhausted that I wanted to get in the cart and ride with the produce. Since I was too pooped to push, I needed a less-energy-consuming shopping solution, which turned out to be a small neighborhood grocery store a block from the Gregory Terrace, at the bottom of Hill Street. Hill Street, indeed. It was a block so steep that I had to carry my groceries to the hotel by walking diagonally back and forth on the sidewalk all the way up the hill.

With few exceptions, my days were routine. Mornings allowed no rolling over for a few extra minutes. I was out from under the covers immediately and into a quick shower, the only place I had any privacy. This was where I would have my private panic attacks, but I didn't allow myself that luxury very often. I was taught to handle a crisis first and then later, when there was time, I could fall apart. In this case, I didn't know when, if ever, there would be a later. After my shower, it was down to the dining room for breakfast. Usually, I ate a big meal because I was never sure what the rest of the day would bring. Then I walked to the hospital, sometimes with someone, often alone.

I stayed at the hospital from 9:00 A.M. to 1:00 P.M., taking my turn sitting with Lani just like everyone else. When the ICU closed between 1:00 and 4:00, it was time for lunch, rest, and any necessary errands. At 4:00 P.M it was back to the hospital until 8:00. After 8:00 P.M. it was home to dinner and bed. If I spent any time before bed relaxing on the sofa, my hip began to ache and I couldn't straighten up when I walked to the bedroom. Falling asleep became a challenge, almost a chore. I learned to pretend I was napping on the sofa at home and imagined sunlight streaming through the windows, falling over me like a warm comforter. I always slept on my side with the blanket up to my chin and my arms tightly crossed over my chest, the only way I knew to protect my heart.

We had created a new family unit with new routines and an unspoken rule that we were each free to take care of ourselves as necessary. If Mickey needed to go off on his own, he went. If Shira needed to be alone with Lani, she was. Shira and Scott went to the ICU in the middle of the night when they couldn't sleep. Louie got up at 5:00 A.M. for a run and stopped first at the hospital to have private time with Lani while the ward was still quiet. I know families that would have turned this into a competition. Someone would be carefully tracking how much time each person spent with Lani, and the one who spent the most time won. I was grateful that was not happening here.

I competed only with my panic. When there were no afternoon errands, I stayed at the hotel and tried to numb my mind by watching terrible daytime TV or playing cards with Shira, while Mickey's method of escape was wandering the city. He went downtown to the Queen Street Mall, and often to the casino at the end of the mall.

One afternoon, he won $100 at the casino, spent it on a pair of walking shoes, wore them once, didn't like how they felt, and gave them to me. I don't know how he got them onto his feet, because they fit me perfectly.

Shira also went out to buy a pair of shoes. She had a terrible time deciding which style she liked but finally came home with a cute pair of sandals. She put them on to model them for us, and discovered, as she looked at her toes curling over the edge, that she'd forgotten to check the size. Our minds were functioning somewhere short of normal.

Shira did make a wise decision when she bought two children's books to read to Lani. Sitting on a tall stool near her sister's head and finishing a story, she whispered, "I don't know what else I can do for you. I want to open my heart and fit you inside for healing and protection. But I'm not sure what you need, so I'm going to keep my heart open and you can use whatever you want. Like the Old Country Buffet Restaurant of support; $6.95 all you can eat."

Mickey came into the ICU, smiled at Shira, and said, "How about I apply rub-on tattoos to Lani. Then when she wakes up she'll think she forgot where she'd had them done."

Shira moaned.

Undaunted in his mission to spread a little cheer, he pulled a racing form out of his pocket. "Lani, I remember what a great handicapper you were. There's a horse here called Rainbow Ribbon. If you think I should bet on him, don't say a thing."

Even the nurses moaned at this one, while Mickey chuckled at what he thought was his stellar sense of humor.

What did cheer us up was the mail we were beginning to receive from home, love and support in little white envelopes, though I noticed Mickey was keeping score to see whose family was sending the most, a behavior, I assumed, created in response to the extreme stress.

Meanwhile, Louie had begun putting together the website to keep family up to date on Lani's progress. He posted a message from us. He scanned a copy of the newspaper article about the accident. When he listed Lani's injuries, Shira insisted he also list her blessings, one of which was her stubbornness. We smiled, knowing Lani would approve. Every evening, Louie updated the site and included photos from his digital camera. Many nights, he fell asleep over his laptop.

The response to the site was overwhelming. It was updated daily with accurate information and pictures, making the process an intimate, technical connection that allowed our family to participate with us in the unfolding drama.

The nurses and doctors loved it, added their comments, and corrected misinformation, explaining that this would become Lani's memory as she recovered. However, Doctor Rothman, a senior staff member doing research on bacteria and antibiotics, saw an ethical issue involved with Lani's right to privacy and insisted on meeting with us one morning in the conference room.

He appeared to be in his late thirties, wore glasses and a full academic beard. I said the chances of anyone not connected to us stumbling onto the website were slim. He persisted. Mickey said it was no different from having visitors in the hospital if the accident had happened at home, and that the connection was important to everyone, including Lani. He was unconvinced. Then Louie suggested that a study of the function of the website in the case history could be a unique paper for Dr. Rothman to write for publication. That snagged his interest. I was furious that this stranger was attempting to limit my communications home, but I did respect that his concerns were ethical as well as medical.

The website stayed up, and Dr. Rothman joined forces with other staff, and used his expertise in antibiotics to make decisions about what drugs Lani needed to fight her infections, her allergy to penicillin adding to the challenge.

Lani had never liked being touched, rarely cuddled, and was uncomfortable with hugs. Now she was trapped on a narrow bed with nurses handling her constantly. I wondered, had she been conscious, how she would react to all this contact. I couldn't acknowledge that it might be only my touch from which she withdrew.

The nurses recorded Lani's vital signs, drained the shunt in her head, wiped her forehead, asked her to open her eyes or squeeze their hands, or push their hands with her foot. Even though she never responded, they kept asking and noted every attempt in her chart which soon grew to three volumes.

The nurses came in every size and shape; tall, short, wide, thin, dark curls, blond with bangs. Libby braided Lani's hair and talked to her when the ward was quiet. Wendy bathed her and shaved her legs. Kirsten checked her stomach contents to see if she were digesting the "food" being pumped into her. Angels with squeaky shoes and charming accents.

Lani's condition was slowly changing. The tubes Dr. Eustas had inserted into her damaged lungs, through incisions under her arms, were removed. They had caused an infection, which was normal, but that made her temperature rise and her brain swelling increase. Once again, the swelling increased the danger of death or permanent brain damage, so she was covered with a cooling blanket to chill her enough to bring down her temperature but not enough to cause her to shiver. Eventually, her temperature and her intracranial pressure began to stabilize, but her face swelled more and more, especially her eyes, especially her left eye. They swelled so much that her lids couldn't cover them, and the intense pressure in her head forced the membranes of her lower lids up and out of her eye sockets, so they lay on her face. All the nurses could do was put ointment on the membranes and cover her entire eye area with plastic wrap to keep them moist and protected.

I could handle no more than one day at a time. Any day I could go to the hospital was a good day. I stood next to Lani's bed, near her head, carefully attentive because of all the wires and tubes. I held her hand and told her about the night before, what we had for dinner, how beautiful the weather was, any trivial thing that came to mind. And, everyday, I saw fresh blood pooled in her ears.

"I love you. You are strong. You are brave. I believe in you. I love you." I repeated every affirming phrase I could think of, believing she could hear me and keep fighting her way back to us. Always at the end of the day, I whispered, "Sweet dreams."

At the end of the week, Luke, a teenage boy was brought into the ICU and put on the bed next to Lani's. We sat on the hallway benches and visited with his parents. They told us that Luke also had been in a car accident, and the friend he had been with had died. Luke was in the ICU for twenty-four hours and then transferred across the hall to Ward 2B. He recovered quickly and, a few days later when he left the hospital, gave us a get well card for our still-unconscious daughter. We did our best to be happy for him, but it was hard to watch Luke walk out into the sunshine with his family and then have to turn around ourselves and walk back into the ICU.

❑

Monday, September 28, 1998

Miracles happen quietly. This morning, when a nurse held Lani's hand and told her to squeeze it, she did. The nurse held Lani's left foot, asked her to push out with her leg. She did. We were summoned from our hallway benches and ushered to her bedside to share the unfolding drama.

"Your mom is holding your hand. Can you squeeze her hand?"

She squeezed my hand. My heart swelled, and I peeked over the edge of my trench.

Mickey, Shira, Louie, and Scott each got a turn getting their hand squeezed. It must have been exhausting for Lani, but she was sharing with us a precious gift, the possibility of a future.

The doctors agreed it was time to repair the fistula and balloon off her dissected left carotid artery. They said the pressure from the fistula was responsible for her eyes' severe swelling and already might have damaged her optic nerve, permanently blinding her left eye. After all she'd been through, blindness in one eye seemed like a relatively small thing. Surgery was scheduled for the next day.

That afternoon, we met with Dr. D'urso in the conference room. He took out his pen and placed a blank piece of paper on the desk in front of him. His back was rigid, his jaw was set, but he looked directly at us, and I knew he would hold nothing back. He began to diagram the complex surgery and list the risks involved.

"The procedure will be as follows: A narrow tube, approximately the width of a guitar string, will be inserted into an artery in Lani's groin area. It will be maneuvered carefully up through her body and through her left dissected carotid artery. This will be a sensitive and tedious procedure, especially because the carotid artery is already damaged."

He paused, looked at us, took a breath, punctuating the danger, and continued. "The tube will continue up into her head until it reaches the fistula. This is where blood is rushing through the tear in the artery behind her left eye and pulsing into a vein. And this is what is causing all the pressure on the optic nerve behind that eye and contributing to the severe facial swelling.

"When the tube reaches the appropriate place, the surgeon will use an electrical pulse to shoot very small titanium coils from the top of the tube into the tear in the artery. With enough coils, he will create a wall and close the tear. Once the coils are in place, they will be permanent. And once these coils are in place, there should be no complications from this part of the surgery. If there are, they will be apparent in the first twenty-four hours."

He scanned our faces to see if we were following him, then checked his notes and continued. "Next, we will balloon off the left dissected artery. Everyone has two carotid arteries and two vertebral arteries that serve the brain. They create what is called the Circle of Willis. A healthy person can live a full life with only three of these arteries functioning. The same procedure will be done with the tube inserted into an artery in the groin area and manipulated again through her body and into her neck.

"We are choosing not to operate on her right carotid artery, hoping that in time it will heal on its own."

He paused and looked around again. "There's danger in passing the first tube through Lani's damaged carotid artery. There's danger that the coils in the fistula behind her eye won't hold or that a coil might slip out of place or be forced out of place by the intense pulsing of the bloodstream and cause a stroke. There's danger that the brain swelling will increase too much during or after the surgery. Questions?"

He looked at each of us. Then he pushed a form across the desk. We stared at it. "It's the release form. Please sign it here." He watched as Mickey and I did what we were told. "She will go into surgery Tuesday between 1:00 and 2:00 P.M. Dr. Mitchell will perform the procedure, and I will assist. It will be long and tedious. At least four or five hours."

He stood, nodded, and left.

We sat in silence.

CHAPTER
Five

Tuesday, September 29, 1998

Before the nurses prepped Lani for surgery, we all gathered around her bed. Scott had wheeled Patrick, finally transferred to Brisbane, into the ICU, where he held Lani's hand and told her dirty jokes. Then he became serious and told her that his sister was coming to Australia to take him back to the States in a few days, and he knew Lani would follow soon.

Her college friends, Ann and Meghan, called from Amherst and, while Scott held the portable phone to Lani's ear, they told her they loved her and that she was going to be fine. After the call, Scott asked her to squeeze twice if she loved her Uncle Louie. She did. Louie stayed steady. We gave her our love and kisses, then we were shooed out so the nurses could get her ready.

We sat in the hall, waiting on our benches, watching the ICU door. When she was finally wheeled out, we could hardly see her through all the tubes, portable monitors, wires and wraps. As the gurney was rolled down the hallway, Shira walked beside it, singing a familiar childhood song to her sister, complete with hand gestures.

"We are going on a hukie lau, on a hukie, hukie, hukie, hukie, hukie lau." At the patient elevator, Shira was turned back.

I stayed on the bench and stared at the wall, my shoulders hunched, my hands folded in my lap. Mickey struck up a conversation with a couple we'd noticed in the past few days visiting Ward 2B.

How does he have the energy to participate in a conversation while I can barely breathe?

He walked them over to me and made introductions.

Oh, please don't. Not now. I smiled and nodded, but I barely looked at them. I have no idea of their age, their size, the color of their hair. I wanted to be left alone.

"Our son is in his early twenties, like your daughter. A few weeks ago he, too, was in a coma in the ICU. The doctors gave us no hope at all, and we had begun to make funeral arrangements for him. While he was being disconnected from all the monitors, a nurse noticed his eyelid move. It was a sign of life, a miracle. He eventually regained consciousness and now he's in Ward 2B. In a few days, we'll be taking him home, and the doctors expect him to make a full recovery. So be strong and believe in miracles. They do happen, and we'll be praying for you and your daughter."

It was a wonderful story and I thanked them for sharing it, but I didn't have the energy to embrace the hope they offered. They tried to throw me a life raft, but it was too far away and the waves in my stormy seas were too high, the water too rough. I was glad when they left and I could go back to waiting in silence.

Mickey left, too. He went back to the hotel to change clothes so he would be ready to go to Kol Nidre service at the synagogue. It was the holiest night of the Jewish year, and the service marked the beginning of Yom Kippur, the Day of Atonement. According to tradition, this was when God decides who will live and who will die, who will be written in the Book of Life for the coming year. It was also the anniversary of the death of Mickey's father. Mickey felt he needed to be in the synagogue for services that evening because it was a holy time and to honor the memory of his father. Shira, torn between comforting both parents, decided to join Mickey so he wouldn't be alone. Dr. Popper planned to pick them up at our waiting post and bring them back after services.

I understand that ritual and ceremony are important and can be soothing, but I saw his decision as a skillful creative avoidance. I could have said, "No, you can't go. You're staying with me at the hospital," but I didn't. I thought we were each doing what we needed to do to get through this experience. But I felt abandoned.

Do you think God can't hear you from the hospital? Do you think your father isn't here, too, watching over Lani? How can you leave me? How can you leave your daughter?

I wouldn't go as far away as the seventh floor cafeteria. That's why I made sandwiches in the morning before we left the hotel. I thought we could eat in the late afternoon without leaving our benches. I was staring at a spot in space when Louie unwrapped one of my creations. He took a bite, paused, and lifted the top slice of bread, then held it out to show me. "Barb, did you consider putting some peanut butter and jelly in the peanut butter and jelly sandwich?"

I remembered putting my knife into the peanut butter jar and the jelly jar, but there was little evidence that I'd ever transferred anything onto the bread. I blinked, looked at his face, then at the sandwich, and giggled despite the tension. "Apparently not."

And so went the entire afternoon. I remember only traces the next five hours and how I got through to the other side of waiting. I tried to distract myself by walking up and down the corridor. I tried sitting in the small waiting room turning pages in old tattered magazines or staring vacantly at the TV screen. Scott spent time on the phone with his mom, and Louie disappeared for a while, to the chapel, I think.

I stayed close, fearing that if I broke my vigil, there would be disaster. Focus was the only way I could think to help my daughter.

Lani, be strong. Doctors, be wise and skilled. My thoughts were prayers, only harder. Why was I so sure it would be my fault if something went wrong? Maybe from years and years of saying "I'm sorry" to everyone, about everything. And so, irrationally, I felt that if I weren't attentive, catastrophe would ensue. So I sat.

At 6:15 P.M., an exhausted Dr. D'urso, still wearing surgical scrubs, appeared in the hallway. Louie slid closer to me on the bench, and Scott leaned in to hear every word.

"Mrs. Greenberg, I am happy to report that both procedures were successful and Lani is doing well.

I lowered my shoulders from my earlobes.

"It took thirteen coils to close the tear in the artery. The surgery is just finishing and your daughter should be brought back to the ICU in an hour or two."

I uncurled my back.

"Then Dr. Mitchell, who performed all the technical and delicate work, will want to talk to you." He nodded and returned to the operating room.

I took a deep breath.

Scott went for the telephones to update his family. Louie stayed close and squeezed my hand. I telephoned Mickey's newly rented cell phone to give him and Shira the news. Services were about to begin, and they would offer prayers of thanks, he said. They planned to be back at the hospital in another two hours. Hopefully, by then, Lani would be back in the ICU. I hung up and closed my eyes. Even with the good report I didn't dare let down my guard. *Stay alert. Be vigilant.* I sat on the bench, seeing nothing for another ninety minutes.

Then, a young man we hadn't seen before breezed out of the ICU giving the immediate impression of a cocky, self-important intern. "Just wanted to let you know your daughter has returned to the ICU and her intracranial pressure is in the seventies." He spoke quickly with a smug smile and then hurried back into the ward.

Seventies. Oh my God! Oh my God! It's supposed to be in the twenties! Oh my God! I tried to look calm, but in my head I was screaming in panic. *What's happening to my daughter? Prepare yourself. Don't think. Hang suspended. Don't make a scene. I don't know if I can survive this.*

After an interminable fifteen minutes, Dr. D'urso came out of the ICU. He was smiling for the first time, and his smile told us everything. I have never seen such a wonderful smile. Relief and joy reflected in his eyes. "She's doing great." He must have seen the remnants of panic on my face in the set of my jaw. "Oh, don't worry about the numbers. The machines always act up when they are reconnected after surgery. She is truly doing great." Still smiling, he turned and walked away.

Without warning, my head fell into my lap as I collapsed against my brother, who wrapped his arms over my back and held me quietly. I saw the young intern who gave us the premature news about the ICP numbers only one other time. He must have been seriously reprimanded because he ducked his head and scurried by. If I hadn't been so well-trained as a nice girl, I would have chased him down the hall and ripped off his face.

Mickey and Shira returned in time for our conference with the head surgeon. Dr. Mitchell looked even more exhausted than Dr. D'urso. He shook our hands firmly and began. "Your daughter is a miracle. It's a miracle she survived the accident, a miracle she survived the helicopter transfer to this hospital, and a miracle she survived the first forty-eight hours and hung on long enough to have this surgery performed." He paused and shook his head in wonderment. "And there is still another miracle. I don't know if you are aware of this, but the procedure used on your daughter is very new. It has been performed in Australia only five other times, and I believe only thirty-five times worldwide." He was proud of what he'd accomplished, but I had a sense he knew that forces greater than his technical skill were at work with his patient.

Mickey and Shira were light and chatty when they were dropped off at the hospital after services. *How dare you? What do you think is going on here?* I couldn't even talk to Mickey. He saw my look and shifted gears, but obviously he didn't get it.

I wanted to plant my fists on my hips and shriek like a fish-wife. *"If you couldn't sit with me during the most terrifying time of our daughter's and my life, you son of a bitch, then at least keep your fucking mouth shut. While you were sitting in a synagogue, I was sitting in a hospital. While you were listening to chanted prayers, I was listening for reports of survival. How dare you come back here and be so insensitive. If you must remove yourself from a difficult situation, then at least respect it when you return. Don't you ever be so self-absorbed around me again. If you can't stand to be here and face the hard stuff, then at least pay attention when you get back."*

But I didn't shriek. I didn't dare. I felt responsible, as if the family took their lead from me, and I needed to be the model of clear, calm, reasonable communication and behavior, so we could survive this. When Lani came back to us, I wanted her to find a family she could still recognize, a family together. There was enough chaos and I didn't want any more. So I stuffed my feelings down deep and chose carefully how I'd speak. Not out of weakness. Maybe out of fear. Certainly I believed out of necessity. It wasn't the time for a self-indulgent outburst, at least not for me.

"You've been at services all evening," I spoke quietly. "You put yourself in a different reality than the rest of us, and you need to be more aware and respectful of what's going on." I told him about the mistaken ICP report from the young doctor. Mickey hugged me and apologized.

There! It was over. I returned his hug out of habit. *What would have happened if I had shrieked? Would that have been a wiser choice? What is going to happen to all of those words I didn't say, the rage I silenced? I can't worry about that now.* My voice had been calm, but the emotion driving the unspoken words was still bitter in my throat and its acid burned in my stomach.

❑

Lani improved daily. The swelling in her face was going down, her eyes started to return to normal size, and the eye membranes receded back into place. She began to look more and more like our daughter. Some days, there was a noticeable difference from our morning hello to our evening goodbye. And she was opening her eyes, blinking to communicate, and squeezing hands. She didn't seem surprised that Mickey, Shira, Louie, Scott, and I were all at her bedside halfway around the world. Even in her coma I believe she'd known we were with her all along. "You were in a car accident," I told her. "You're going to be fine. We're all here. We love you."

In the days before her operation, the nurses were aware that Lani might not survive and had wisely and compassionately let us all stay near her without any restrictions. But after the operation, they began strict enforcement of the ICU rule of only two visitors at a time per patient; a signal that our daughter was healing.

The increased activity around her bed was another sign. Therapists came daily to pound on her chest, forcing her into coughing spasms that cleared her lungs. Nurses asked Louie and me to assist with the physical therapy of slowly stretching and bending Lani's legs, her feet, and her good arm to keep her muscles from atrophying.

Dr. D'urso checked on her often, and the more she improved, the larger his smile became. He decided to remove the shunt from her head before it could cause an infection. He met with us in the conference room and proudly showed us the new CAT scan of Lani's brain. He showed us her two skull fractures, the strategically placed titanium coils, the closed off left carotid artery, and the damaged right one.

He said he hoped the right artery would heal without intervention, but until then there'd be a risk of a stroke, so he was putting Lani on a heavy dose of blood-thinning medication.

"As she becomes increasingly alert, you may notice personality changes. Commonly, patients become less inhibited or have more of a temper."

"That's our Lani," I said, smiling with anticipation of having her back.

"You've just described my sister," Shira added.

Mickey laughed. "If those are the changes, we probably won't even notice."

❑

Friday, October 2, 1998

Today, Lani was to have a second surgery, and Dr. D'urso was again making a list for us. His face was softer than before, more open. A good sign. A good face.

"This is a two-fold operation. First is a tracheostomy. She is still not breathing on her own, but if the ventilator tubes stay down her throat much longer, they could create permanent damage to her vocal chords. As you know, the tubes supply air to her lungs and nourishment into her stomach. So first we'll make a small incision at the base of her trachea through which we'll insert a narrow tube that will connect to the respirator and keep her breathing artificially. Then we'll put a feeding tube up her nose that will curve through the sinus cavity to the back of her throat, so she can continue to be fed, through the back door, so to speak. Finally, her broken arm will need to be set. The orthopedic surgeon will give you the details on that procedure. Do you have any questions for me?"

He looked at each of us. "No? Sign the release form here." The form still looked dangerous, but the air in the room felt less heavy.

The orthopedic surgeon. He was young and athletic, looking as if he came directly from a workout at the gym. He explained the procedure on her arm: "The forearm has two main bones. The longer bone on the outside arm is broken, cracked in half. As a result, the shorter bone, on the inside of her forearm has been ripped out of its socket. The broken bone will be put back together and held in place with a metal plate and six to eight screws on each side of the break. Then the smaller bone will need to be rotated back into place. The procedure will take approximately one-and-a-half hours. We hope there will be no nerve damage, and after physical therapy, she should regain motion of her arm."

❏

The surgery was scheduled for 1:00 P.M., and again we waited on the hard, wooden benches. We watched a tiny, smiling woman in a white blouse and pale blue skirt, accompanied by a teenage girl, carry a bouquet of flowers down the faded hallway to the ICU and ring the bell.

Don't they know flowers aren't allowed in the ICU, and there's no visiting in the afternoon? I was mildly irritated and my hip hurt.

The woman spoke to someone who answered the ICU door. Then she turned away and walked to the pay phones. Mickey hadn't fled the scene of this operation and he overheard her conversation. When she hung up he asked, "Do you have someone in the ICU named Lane?"

Her smile broadened and she nodded.

"That's a coincidence. Our daughter is also in the ICU and her name is Lani"

"Oh! That's the name. Lani!"

I snapped to attention.

"And...Oh, my...you're her parents. I'm Lorraine." She held the bouquet in front of her with both hands, like a tense bride. Her voice was excited and breathless. "I'm a registered nurse. I was in the car right behind your daughter when the accident happened, and I was the first one down the hill to the crash. I turned off the car engine and then climbed up on the boot. What do you Americans call it? The trunk. I climbed up on the trunk and looked through the rear window. It was shattered, totally shattered, and it was the only way I could reach the children," she continued in a rush.

"I saw that Lani's injuries were the worst. There was so much blood. Her head was lying against Patrick's shoulder and I knew she couldn't breathe in that position, so I lifted her head. Then I shouted for someone to bring me a towel to support her neck and I held her until the ambulance came. She was unconscious, but I talked to her and told her to breathe more slowly. I think she heard me somehow because her breathing calmed."

Lorraine inhaled, her eyes wide, her adrenaline pumping, reliving the rescue.

A guardian angel had followed my Lani.

"You saved her life," I whispered. "Thank you." I hugged Lorraine fiercely, my eyes filling with tears. "Thank you, thank you." I should be saying something else to her. I didn't know what else to say. The nightmare of my daughter lying alone in the grass wasn't true. This angel had arrived to watch over her.

Meeting this petite wonder who saved my daughter's life was the closest I'd come so far to falling apart. She was the first in a series of people who'd saved Lani, but if Lorraine hadn't been there and held Lani's head...*Dear God.* I overwhelmed her with another hug and then we sat down to hear more details. Lorraine shared eagerly.

"The Ford Falcon was being driven very erratically. I was driving behind it and wanted to pass, but I didn't dare. I saw the collision and the little red car fly out of control and plunge into the ditch. I pulled over immediately and ran to help. When I got to the car, I could hear Emily moaning in the front seat. Patrick was covered in blood, his and Lani's." She stopped to catch her breath.

"After the ambulance took Lani and Emily, I stayed with Patrick. You see, his foot was pinned in the car and he couldn't move. I just talked with him and did my best to reassure him everything would be all right. I wasn't going to leave that young man alone. And the police, they were wonderful. You know, they tried for ninety minutes to get dear Patrick out of that wreck. They finally had to use a big contraption they called the jaws-of-life to pull the car apart so Patrick could be freed. When they started up that machine, I still wouldn't leave so they threw this huge tarp over both of us to protect us from pieces of glass and metal. And my, what a terrible noise that was."

Lorraine paused and flushed, "Oh, I haven't introduced you to my daughter, Lisa. Lisa smiled and shook our hands. She was a younger version of her mother, small, with the same shoulder-length, light brown hair and warm smile. "Lisa here is seventeen, almost eighteen. My husband, Keith, and I have six more children at home. Lisa is our oldest, and our youngest is just turning four. It's a handful but we love 'em."

And I love you, Lorraine. Blessings to you forever.

As we visited, a nurse peeked his head out of the ICU. "The surgery has gone very well, but patients always look shitty after they return to us from an operation." He grinned. We'd become so close to everyone in the ICU that we spoke to each other like family, and I loved that his comments were genuine because they meant Lani was fine.

"It's going to be another five to ten minutes before you can see your daughter," he said before disappearing back into the ward with a wink.

"Let us translate for you," Mickey explained. "Five to ten minutes in ICU time means thirty minutes out here in the hallway."

"No worries." Lorraine smiled. "Lisa and I can wait." Lorraine filled the time with stories of her children, and Lisa talked about looking forward to graduating high school. As Lorraine told us about her home, we realized it must have taken her at least two hours to drive here for this visit.

After thirty minutes, we got the okay from the nurse, and Lorraine joined us at Lani's bedside. Lani was still sedated and the trachea hole was fresh and raw. Lorraine took Lani's hand and reintroduced herself to the young woman whose life she'd saved. Background music should have swelled, a golden glow should have surrounded the bed and its holy visitor. But it was an ordinary scene for the ICU.

How often so much is hidden in the ordinary. Sacred moments and gestures, not hidden at all, simply not seen for what they really are.

Lorraine and Lisa returned to visit on Monday, Lisa's eighteenth birthday. Shira bought a chocolate cake, a carrot cake, and a box of candles. Our entire gang, Mickey, Shira, Louie, Scott, and I escorted Lorraine and her daughter to the hospital cafeteria, pushed two tables together, and had a birthday party.

What am I doing singing "Happy Birthday" in the seventh floor cafeteria?

It's a reminder, Barb. Your daughters each have birthdays in a week. Celebrate. It's safe now. Maybe.

CHAPTER
Six

Sunday, October 4, 1998

Lani was communicating with her eyes when she had the strength to open them. Serious eyes. *"Thank you."* Intense eyes. *"I love you."* I heard her clearly as she looked at me and responded in kind.

Can you hear me, dear child, when I say with my eyes how much I love you?

Shira was the one who understood her sister the best. The two carried on long, wordless conversations. Shira could read the subtle changes in Lani's face and in her eyes. "You can't understand why your left eye won't open?" Lani responded silently, clearly. "Your eye is open. It's already open. Because of the injury to your head, you can't see out of it any more," Shira said gently. "You are blind in your left eye."

Lani stared at Shira. As she had come out the coma in the past few days, she had slowly become aware that she was flat on her back, able to move only her legs and one arm slightly. She could hear voices around her, and machines beeping, but she couldn't speak, and now she was told she had lost the sight in one eye. She couldn't scream in anguish, stomp out of the room in a rage, or slam a door. She could only lie in silence. She never told us how she felt to hear this news for the first time, and I never asked. To do so would be to intrude without permission too far into her heart.

We were all trying to contribute to her recovery, but there was so little we could do. Shira read children's books to her and stories about Brad Pitt from *People* magazine. With the nurses' permission, she bought a radio to put near Lani's head so her sister could listen to music. Louie worked on his website. Mickey did research and found an attorney to work with us. Scott took over the husband role, which was very uncomfortable at first for Mickey and Shira because they hardly knew him. It didn't bother me because he was medicine for Lani. My antenna was focused exclusively on her. That was my job, my contribution, and I never left my post. I guarded her whether I stood by her bed, sat on the wooden bench, or rested at the Gregory Terrace. I draped my soul over her and covered her wounds with my spirit. I never left her.

My guardian role was enough for me, but Mickey ached to do more. He wanted to bring order out of chaos, to control the situation. But he couldn't. Even the doctors' and nurses' resources were limited. The outcome was up to God and Lani.

In desperation, Mickey took action, controlling what he could. He started by reorganizing the files of all our e-mails and letters. Then he took over our address book. Next, he dominated our conversations, not bothering to listen to Shira or me. Then he moved on to all our decisions and choices. Not medical ones, but where to eat, when to leave, how to spend our afternoons, whether to walk or take a cab. Prince Charming run amuck, plowing over the princess instead of sweeping her off her feet.

Shira was confused by his behavior, and I continued to rationalize, assuming he was creating behaviors to help him survive the situation, like the day of the first surgery, when he abandoned me in the ICU hallway. Now he'd left me again on his quest to be in charge. I didn't have enough physical and emotional reserve to confront what he was doing, so I let it happen by default. Does that make me complicit? I believe it does.

❑

Wednesday, Shira and I were at Lani's side when she tried for the first time to communicate by forming a word with her mouth.

"Wh...."

We began to guess. "What happened?"

No, she blinked.

"Where am I?"

No.

"Where is Scott?"

No.

She was getting frustrated and tired.

A nurse saw us struggling to understand. "Oh, she wants water, don't you, Lani?

Yes.

"Well, I can't give you water, but I can give you a wet cloth to suck on."

Yes.

The next morning, my inability to interpret my daughter's need hit me. I stood crying in the shower once more, wishing the hot water would rinse away my failure, but it stayed deeply embedded in my skin like a fine, sharp sliver of glass. I was supposed to guard her, but I couldn't even understand what she wanted. I should have known. Mothers are *supposed* to know these things. *I'm terrible. I'm worthless.*

Then, embarrassed at my weakness, I turned off the water and toweled off so I could get dressed and get to my post on time, determined not to fail again, but knowing I probably would.

That's how life is. Mistakes, fumbling, tripping, spilling. Those aren't bad things. They're how we learn. They make life colorful, interesting, real. But I don't like them, and now especially, they're unacceptable.

❏

Thursday afternoon, Mickey forced me out of my strict routine by insisting I go with him and Louie to a park near the Brisbane River, on the edge of downtown where a carnival was in progress. It was a hot day and the sun felt good, like a warm hand on my back. We walked by booth after booth of food vendors, bringing back memories of the Minnesota State Fair and buckets of French fries, cheese curds, mini donuts, and corn dogs. We stopped to order exotic fried fish sandwiches for lunch, sat on a shaded spot of grass, and watched the people: parents with small children, giggling teenagers, young couples and old, enjoying the day.

After our picnic, Louie left to run errands and simply have time alone. Mickey and I walked slowly down a path near the river. We had escaped for an afternoon into a lovely scene where large trees shaded us as we gazed across the water. There was a marina on the far shore, and a few small boats cruised by. Until now, being outside consisted of walking back and forth to the hospital, up and down the hill, listening to traffic, and smelling exhaust. But here it was so quiet, and the green scent of the trees mixed with the damp smells from the water; childhood smells of splashing in a lake or rolling in the grass of a neighbor's backyard. Smells from when I felt safe.

I began to let down my guard. The tension in my back lessened, as did the ache in my hip. As we turned a corner, we passed a young woman in a wheelchair. She might have been Lani's age. She was leaning awkwardly to one side, eyes blank, mouth open slightly, legs covered with a blanket, arm bent tightly to her chest, hand curled stiffly. As her parents pushed her chair past us, my legs buckled as they had that first night in the ICU. Mickey led me to a bench where I sat and stared at the water and cried. We sat together on that bench until it was time to return to the hospital.

❏

Monday, October 5, 1998

Lani was sitting up. Rather, the bed raised her to a partial sitting position. The nurses only allowed her to remain upright for a few minutes, but it was a miracle. She was a miracle! She was raising her eyebrows, squeezing hands, moving her legs. She was being weaned off the respirator and breathing on her own. After she'd spent two full nights off the respirator, Dr. D'urso transferred her into 2B, the ward down the hall. The staff told us not to be too disappointed if she had to return to the ICU once or twice; that wasn't unusual.

"What does this mean? Is she out of the woods?" we asked.

"She's not out of the woods yet, but she is standing right on the edge," Dr.D'urso assured us with his largest grin yet.

The next day, Lani's hair was washed. Then she was dressed in a fresh yellow hospital gown and wheeled out of the ICU. Louie walked along side her gurney taking pictures and Scott covered her ceremoniously with Baubie's blanket. The rest of us cheered softly to avoid disturbing her new neighbors in 2B.

During our celebration, the ICU nurses confided to Shira that before Mickey and I had arrived form the States they'd also put a fresh gown on Lani and brushed her hair back neatly on the pillow. That time they had been sure it would be the last time we'd see our daughter alive. Now they considered Lani their Minnesota Miracle.

I still can't admit that our daughter might have died, though certainly I had glimpses. The possibility is too awful, and it's not in the rule book. Well, it is in the rule book, but it shouldn't be.

After Lani was settled and tucked in for the night, we celebrated with dinner at a charming restaurant, Eve's on the River. I ordered a big bowl of pasta, my favorite comfort food, and topped it off with a steaming cup of hot chocolate. The river sparkled under the full moon, as if stars had been floated on the surface of the water to make them easier to wish upon.

The next morning, we inspected ward 2B thoroughly. It was a long, narrow, open ward, with beds against both walls, and blue privacy curtains that could be drawn between each bed. Close to one end of the ward was the nurses' station, and just beyond that, the patients' lavatories and showers. Beyond the nurses' station were also six more beds for patients who needed extra care and supervision. These beds were tended by three nurses, one nurse for every two patients. This was Lani's new home.

The first nurse we met was Lonnie who was petite and had a huge smile. Next, we met the head nurse. She was not petite, did not smile, and informed us which afternoon hours we were not allowed into the ward. No exceptions.

Lani lay in her new bed with a bandage covering the spot on her head where the shunt had been, a thin feeding tube in her nose, a neck brace with an opening to accommodate the tracheotomy tube, and a heavy cast on her left arm that had to be supported on a pillow. She was not attached to a machine. The wires were gone. There was no beeping. And the silence was a promise of healing to come.

This morning, Lani was helped out of bed by two nurses. Her face was white from the intense pain in her head caused by the movement, but she managed a brief smile. She'd been flat on her back for two weeks and she recognized the power of this simple activity. Her shoulders hunched forward, her legs were skin and bone, but with one nurse on each side, holding her, Lani took three steps away from the bed and three steps back. She repeated this amazing feat again and again that afternoon, and the next day the nurses walked her all the way to the bathroom—a major accomplishment.

The staff was dedicated, and the care was exceptional. Even so, one night when Lani had to go to the bathroom, the only way she could get the attention of a nurse was to bang her feet against the edge of the bed. And the next morning, thinking she might like some privacy, a nurse left her alone on the toilet, but Lani got dizzy and collapsed onto the concrete floor. The road to recovery is frustrating and frightening, but it's still the best road.

Assorted therapists began arriving at Lani's bedside daily. Physical therapists massaged her chest to make sure her lungs were strong and clear. Sometimes as her lungs tried to expel phlegm, she had coughing spasms that shook her body violently. Until she was strong enough to cough out the congestion on her own, a nurse helped Lani by suctioning out her airway mechanically through a narrow tube inserted into the trach hole.

A speech therapist came to see how Lani's vocal chords were healing. Because the respirator tubes had damaged her throat, the therapist prescribed thick drinks to restore Lani's swallowing reflexes. I added powdered chocolate to this mutant liquid and we'd pretend they were thick chocolate milk or chocolate pudding. But they definitely weren't.

Lani was desperate for a drink of water, but her therapist wouldn't allow it. Sitting by Lani's bedside, hands primly folded in her lap, she explained. "Water is harder to swallow than thick liquid and if you swallow wrong and the water gets into your lungs, you could develop pneumonia. Before you can have any water," the therapist said sympathetically, "you have to show me you can swallow."

Lani took this as a challenge. She looked at the therapist, focused, closed her mouth, swallowed consciously and carefully three times, three big gulps, then opened her mouth wide and stuck out her tongue. We laughed. Lani was back and she was ready. The therapist was amazed but still cautious, so it would be awhile before Lani's request was granted.

Lani's communication with us was still wordless, but she now was given a board printed with letters of the alphabet. One of us would hold it near her right hand, and with all the strength she could muster, she would point to letters, slowly, tediously, spelling out words.

I...N...E...E...D...T...O...

"I need to"

S...I...T...U...P...S...O

"Sit up so."

"I need to sit up so. So what, honey?"

M...Y...H...E...A...D...C...A...N...

"I need to sit up so my head can. You're doing great, go on..."

A...D...J...

We looked nervously at each other. A, D, J, maybe something is wrong.

...U...

This wasn't spelling a word. Something is wrong.

"Adjust, adjust!" Shira cried out. "She wants to sit up so she can adjust her head."

Lani blinked and closed her eyes, exhausted.

Adjust. What a great word.

As she gained her strength, Lani graduated from the alphabet to an erasable children's board that the nurses had found for her. Often when we visited, the bed was adjusted so that she was sitting up, her head supported by pillows, with the writing board on her lap and her Baubie's blanket beside her. One morning to amuse her, Mickey stood at the foot of the bed with a small stuffed koala on his head.

"Dad is crazy," Lani wrote. Louie put a picture of Mickey on the website labeled, "Koala with Mickey up its ass."

Dr. D'urso approached and we sobered immediately, but he just smiled at his patient. "Lani, you're a miracle." He was proud and protective of her. "I know you have terrible pain in your head. In the same way that your arm hurts because it was broken, you head will hurt because it was broken, too. But it's healing, and you are healing. And don't despair when depression hits, because it will. That's part of the healing process, too. The dark feelings will pass. It will take time, but you will be whole again."

She looked intently at his face, absorbing every word. She trusted him and he honored her trust. There was always a moment of silence after Dr. D'urso left us, even when he had good news.

Then Lani wrote on her board, "people's letters." She loved hearing us read the cards and letters she was receiving, so we kept a boxful by her bed. Twice, she wrote the name of her horseback riding coach. Where was her letter? The letter from the woman who for six years had been a second mother to her? The fine trainer who taught Lani how to handle not only her horse but the emotional highs and lows that came with intense competition. This woman knew about the crash and about Lani's condition, but we never heard from her.

I pictured her, long-legged in her jeans, leaning against the white fencing of a riding ring and I wanted to scream. *How could you cause my daughter such pain? She loved you and idolized you and you can't send her a fucking get well card! What's wrong with you?*

I was furious. My anger towards Lani's trainer was greater than it was towards the phantom driver from the youth hostel. I knew her. We'd spoken together, laughed together, and I paid her bills when they came. She was real, and her callous behavior was deliberate, not accidental. Maybe she did me a favor by giving me a safely distant target for my pain. Raging at misfortune was pointless and raging at Mickey felt dangerous, so I raged at this faraway woman, determined to wallow in my resentment. It felt good not to be nice. I looked at Lani and had to shake my head. No card from your coach.

After reading a few letters, Lani was tired, so we left for the afternoon. That evening when we returned, she was eager to communicate. She looked at Mickey and wrote.

"Remember when you put your hands on my head and blessed me before I left on my trip?" It was a tradition that Mickey had performed since the girls were very young. Every Friday night before the Sabbath began and before we sat down for dinner, he put his hands on our daughters' heads and repeated a Hebrew blessing.

He nodded, puzzled.

She erased her board and began again. "I believe that blessing saved my life."

Looking stunned, he stared at her silently, and then was abnormally quiet for the rest of the evening. Later, back at the hotel, he sat very still in his chair. "What greater gift can a father give to his daughter? There is nothing greater," he murmured. Then he noticed me. "Barb, do you feel bad?"

"Yes, a little," I shrugged.

He nodded, but I didn't believe for a minute that he understood why.

Why didn't I tell the truth? Do I feel bad? Of course I do! You're her hero? You, who goes off gambling and shopping, who leaves during her surgery? I'm the one who stays. What about me? I'm the one who stays.

Now that Lani was communicating, another therapist began to come regularly to determine if she had any brain damage. At their first meeting the therapist asked the most ridiculous questions. Standard, I suppose, but stupid.

"What day is it?"

How should she know? I hardly know.

Lani pointed to Thursday on the therapist's sheet printed with days of the week. The therapist sighed acknowledging the incorrect answer and Shira came to her sister's defense. "We watched the TV show "90210" last night. In the states that program is on Wednesday night. So that is why Lani is assuming today is Thursday."

Shira's reward for her input was to be banished from Lani's bedside until the questioning was over, and she left glaring violently at the therapist.

"What time is it?"

Are you joking?

I didn't dare open my mouth lest I be removed also.

"When is your birthday?" Lani was to point to the answer on a sheet of paper with numbers 1 through 9, but her birthday was October 10. 10/10. There were no zeroes on the paper.

Aw, give me a break.

CHAPTER
Seven

Thursday, October 8, 1998

In two days, Lani would be a miraculous 22 years old. And Shira would turn 26 tomorrow, the same day Louie was returning to the States. Louie, Mickey, and I spent the afternoon quickly buying birthday presents and a giant thank-you basket of chocolates for the ICU staff. Mickey and I found the same gift to give each daughter in an art gallery a block from the Queensland Street Mall. We bought them each an emu egg almost five inches high and painted with traditional Aboriginal designs representing life.

That evening, we had a special dinner to honor my brother's last night with us. It was hard to say goodbye. I would miss his gentle presence and his quiet strength. Simply getting ready to go out exhausted me, even though all I did was take off my jeans and T-shirt and put on my sundress, comb my hair, and put on lipstick that I dug up from the bottom of my purse. By the time we got to the restaurant, I could barely keep my head from falling on the table, a position that was getting familiar.

The next day, after Louie left, Scott moved into our apartment, and we celebrated Shira's birthday that evening by ordering pizza from room service and having a picnic on the living room floor.

In the morning, we entered 2B and found Lani sitting in a chair next to her bed, dressed in a fresh blue hospital gown. We sang "Happy Birthday" and she eagerly opened her presents, one-handed. She'd always wanted to learn to play a guitar, so Scott gave her one in blazing cobalt blue. She grinned at the gift, so confident of healing. Shira found a guitar case lined with thick purple shag fabric and a floral guitar strap in electric yellow and shocking pink. Scott had made a dream catcher to hang over her bed, and told how he'd cut a branch from bushes near the hotel, purchased beads in a shop downtown, and spent part of each evening threading its designs.

Our angel-of-the-accident, Lorraine, appeared and joined the celebration, bringing both girls Christian crosses on chains. A new experience for my nice Jewish girls who were deeply aware these were gifts from the heart, a blessing of love, healing, and protection.

Lani tired quickly, so we left her with Shira watching "Days of Our Lives" reruns on the TV. As we walked to the door, I turned to look at our daughters. In the glance, I grasped two things: first, the world is a more dangerous place than I had ever dreamed, and second, there are more miracles here on Earth than I ever imagined. We'd been told that Lani's recovery process would take at least a year, but her speedy progress was a triumph of the human spirit, of the power of prayer, of the magic of medical science, and of the strength of family.

I looked around the ward. Most of the patients were elderly, but I was intensely aware of two teenage boys in nearby beds. One had been transferred into 2B a few days after Lani. His mother sat with him daily. He didn't respond to outside stimuli, and he needed to be physically restrained with thick straps on his arms and legs because he often thrashed uncontrollably.

The other boy had dark hair and big brown eyes with beautiful long, thick lashes. On the wall near his bed someone had hung his football jersey and pictures of his teammates and friends. His parents came every day to be with him, rub his legs, and stretch his muscles. They said he had been hurt initially playing football. A few days later, he had lost consciousness while driving his car and crashed. Every day, the nurses sat him in a chair. Some days his beautiful eyes were vacant, while others they were brighter, sparkling, as if his mind were close to opening to the world again. He had been in the ward over ninety days.

We are blessed. I'm so grateful. This is more than a miracle. The parting of the Red Sea and walking on water are nothing compared to the return of my daughter. This is so big that I can't wrap my mind around it. I could say it's because she is strong, and the doctors are wise, and family and friends prayed, but it's seductive to think we have all the answers. I look at these boys. I'm sure they're strong, and their families and friends love and pray for them, and their doctors are excellent. So, how can I rationalize that my daughter is recovering and they're not?

I walked back to the hotel alone. The sun was hot, the wind was strong in my face, the hill was steep. The gray in my hair wasn't colored. The pallor of my face wasn't hidden with makeup. The eight-dollar dress I wore wasn't really mine. I was just a tired old woman trudging up a hill as women have done for generations. I was unaware of traffic or buildings, only the hill. An old woman with a burden, trudging up a hill one step at a time. I was any woman, in any country, at any time, following the footprints of other mothers carrying a burden of loss and pain. I was worn down to my core: a small round enduring stone.

The day after Lani's birthday, twenty days after the collision, when we first saw our daughter tangled in wires and guarded by machines, her trach tube was removed and Darth Vadar entered our lives.

"Luke, I am your father." She spoke to us in a husky whisper that was to be her voice until her vocal cords healed. She grinned and we laughed, and when I bent over to kiss her good night, she whispered a hoarse, "Sweet dreams," returning to me the words I'd left her with for so many evenings.

But dreams were no longer an issue for her. Lani was focused on recovering. Her impatience, a volatile thing when she was a child and a driving force when she was a teenager, now fueled her determination to heal. She walked alone to the bathroom even though she got dizzying head rushes simply sitting up in bed. She took short wheelchair rides down the hall, not having the strength to sit up for more than a few minutes at a time. She never complained, though it was clear that the pain in her head was agony, and we had to time her pain pills carefully. She was demonstrating true courage, the courage to believe in the essence of self without limitation. She was resolved to regain herself, reclaim herself. She overwhelmed me.

Other than the cast on her arm, the only remaining artificial accessory was the slender feeding tube in her nose and, depending on how much solid food she ate, it, too, would soon be gone. She did her best to eat the meals provided: three mounds of mush, one orange, one green, and one white, and of course the ever-present thick chocolate drink. We tried to create some variety by sneaking in a McDonald's hot fudge sundae one day and a cheeseburger and fries the next. Like most of us, she had no trouble with the sundae, but the cheeseburger and fries were harder. She had to take small bites and chew with intense concentration, but in the end, not a fry was left. That tube was looking at its last days.

Exhausted after her meal, she would lie back in bed as Scott adjusted the pillows for her head. He was a treasure, usually returning to the hospital alone at 9:30 or 10:00 every evening to have private time with Lani. This was an act of courage as well as love because his walks coincided with dinnertime for the large fox bats of the neighborhood. During the day, they slept unnoticed high in the trees. At night, they swooped low into the park searching for their evening meal. Their flight pattern always took them across Scott's path. He tried walking on different sides of the street. He braved the traffic and tried walking in the street. It didn't matter. He couldn't avoid them, so he simply ducked and ran.

Scott and Lani's late-night rendezvous may have been romantic, but I doubted they were kissing, because one of the side effects of having tubes down her throat for two weeks was that she had developed thrush, a fuzzy, bright green, very-contagious fungus that coated her tongue making it look like something left too long in the back of the refrigerator.

But they laughed, talked, and cried, all excellent medicines for healing. I was grateful to Scott because I hadn't seen Lani cry since the accident. I wondered if she worried that seeing her tears would cause us more pain, or if she was protecting herself from our fumbling efforts to ease her grief.

Wednesday afternoon, Lani had an unexpected visitor. Missy Zlotaca, a horseback-riding friend from high school whom Lani hadn't seen in five years, appeared, blonde and bubbly, at her bedside. Missy was studying in Australia and had heard about Lani's accident through friends in the States. She took a twenty-three-hour train ride to Brisbane, planning to spend three days sightseeing in the mornings and visiting with Lani every afternoon. To pass the time, Lani showed Missy photos she had taken during her travels prior to the crash. For each picture, Lani wrote on her board where the photo was taken and what was happening during that part of the trip, remembering details and expressing herself clearly. Writing was still less tiring than speaking, but however she communicated, she confirmed what we all sensed: her mind was not damaged. She had returned to us completely. All of her.

After Missy returned to school, newly scheduled medical procedures were all that disrupted our routine. One evening, when Lani was wheeled away for another set of x-rays, Shira, Scott, and I went with her. To pass the time while she lay waiting on the gurney, Scott blew up a nurse's latex glove and pretended to play ball. Lani took the glove from him, put it under her hospital gown so she looked pregnant and whispered, "How my trip to Australia changed my life!" Picking up the fantasy, Scott tried to deliver the balloon baby, but Lani made it a difficult delivery and wouldn't let go. We laughed so hard that a nurse came marching sternly down the hall to reprimand us.

Two days later, an x-ray technician looked at Lani's chart. "I remember when they brought you in the first night you were here. We didn't understand why the doctors wanted to take x-rays. It seemed like a waste of time. You looked so bad we didn't think you'd make it. Glad you did."

My stomach dropped. I couldn't tell how Lani processed that remark, and I didn't know how to ask.

❏

Monday, October 12, 1998

Lani's bed was moved to the veranda, a section of the ward we hadn't noticed because it was around a corner and out of the direct sight of the nurses' station. At one time, it might have been an actual veranda where recovering patients strolled with their families on bright afternoons. Now, the wide hallway was lined with the overflow of hospital beds separated by familiar blue curtains, and a few narrow windows let in sunshine and a view of the exterior wall of another wing of the hospital.

The move signaled Lani's improvement, and her therapists seemed inspired to work even more conscientiously to determine any level of brain damage by asking her increasingly complex questions.

"Lani, if you went into a grocery store, what would you get?"

"Well, first a loaf of bread, peanut butter, jelly, and milk. I love PBJ's. Then I'd get macaroni and cheese for my sister. Of course, ice cream, the kind that has the hot fudge swirled right in it." She went on and on, and I watched the therapist's eyes glaze.

Scott was determined to help her strengthen her body, taking on the job of coach. "Walk a few more steps. One more. You can do it. One more. That's the ticket. One more. Great job."

And I wanted to protect her. "Don't push too hard. Don't go too far. You don't have to rush anything."

Lani laughed at us. She'd do what felt right for her no matter what we said. It was her body. She listened to it and trusted herself to do what was in her own best interest.

Scott took her for her first long walk through the ward and down the hall to 4B/ICU. He rang the bell to announce their arrival, and when the door opened and the nurses saw Lani, they cheered and rushed to greet her.

"You're standing up. It's Ilana, our Minnesota miracle!"

"You're so tall!"

"You're beautiful!"

Lani grinned, apologizing, "I'm so sorry, but I don't remember you at all."

"No worries, hon. We're used to that. Our patients are usually unconscious when they're with us!"

"You've got one great guy there," indicating Scott, who blushed.

"Come see us again!"

"We're so proud of you!"

"You're doing great!"

"You look wonderful."

"We want to see you again!"

The nurses returned to their duties, and carefully, tentatively, Lani turned and with Scott's help, shuffled back to her bed where she laid down and closed her eyes. Her walk must have felt like a victory and I wondered if, through the pain in her head, she was glimpsing past rowing triumphs, finishing races aching and dizzy, sweaty and exhilarated. Or did she remember early morning workouts on the river with the sun just rising, catching sight of an eagle gliding across the sky. She and her teammates trained daily to row faster and be stronger, shoulders and legs straining, lungs hungry for air and nauseous from the lack of oxygen, palms bleeding and blistering on the oars. She was never afraid to push through pain to reach a goal. I do know that she decided, while lying in her bed on the veranda that she would speak at the Crew Banquet in March, to explain to her peers how this sport can change a life, how it can can save a life.

❑

Some months later, back home, Mickey and I were at a dinner party and there was talk about a college basketball scandal. One of the guests, an academic snob, complained about the absurdity of college sports. Clearly, he couldn't know that sports can teach more about life than anything you can read in a book or dissect in a lab. You can study literature and history, calculus and computer science, and learn your subjects well. But they can't teach you how to win graciously, because you won't always win, or how to lose a game without losing heart. You won't learn how to focus under pressure, to persist when you're scared and doubting, to get up when you fall down. Many of us lead narrow lives, timid lives, because we were never taught these lessons.

But at that dinner party, silent Barbara said nothing, and it bothered me for days. By not speaking my truth in Australia, I had edited myself back into extinction. I had grabbed hold of old habits, bad habits, like a reformed smoker lighting up again. I didn't think the damage would be life-threatening, but my silence settled in my soul, a suffocating betrayal.

❑

There were times when I would leave the hospital and catch my breath for a moment. Shira and Mickey would take me on outings; we would walk the Queensland Street Mall and buy ice cream cones and check out tourist gift shops crowded with stuffed koala bears, T-shirts, baseball caps, key chains, and coasters. In one small store, I was attracted to a basket of rings, all narrow bands, inlaid with pieces of sea shells, looking like blue-green mother of pearl. At only a dollar each, I treated myself to three, thinking I could wear them stacked together to look like a wide band. Back at the hotel, I realized they looked terrible together, but Shira had a plan. She slipped one back on my finger, the second on her finger, and put the third in her pocket to take to the hospital for Lani to wear. We three Greenberg girls were committed to each other. I was the proud mother of two grown women, each with their own unique voice, who said how they felt and trusted what they knew. How did that happen? How could I pass on something I didn't have? Maybe it was grace. Maybe it was magic. Maybe it was another miracle. I decided my one-dollar ring was never going to leave my finger.

The day after my purchase, Ann and Jim arrived from the States and knocked on our apartment door. Ann was a dear friend from the horse world. I had phoned her the morning of the accident, knowing she and her husband would be traveling in Australia and hoping they would know people we could contact once we arrived. They did not, but Ann had kept close tabs on us since then. Although their original destination was the southern city of Adelaide, they took a two-thousand-mile detour to spend one day in Brisbane with us. Jim, tall, with salt-and-pepper hair, visited with Mickey at the dining room table while Ann, a petite powerhouse with short brown hair and big brown eyes, sat close to me on the sofa. "Barb, how are you doing? I get updates on Lani all the time from the website, and I want to know about you. How are you?"

"I'm okay. I'm fine. A little weary, but I'm just fine." I sighed and turned my new ring on my finger.

"You're looking good, you really are," she said with an encouraging squeeze of my hand. It was interesting that so little of the horror had registered on my face. Most had settled deep in my body like an iceberg, with only a fraction showing in my eyes, and the rest hidden, massively threatening beneath the surface. If that iceberg ever melted, we'd have a flood of biblical proportions.

We escorted Ann and Jim to the hospital, and Lani lit up when she saw fresh faces, her social circle having been rather limited. She had met Jim once before, and she knew Ann well from horseback riding. Jim stood while Ann sat on a chair close to Lani's head. Of all the gifts Ann brought, the best was her horse show gossip. There's nothing like it. It's distracting, delicious, and of absolutely no value. "No one's heard much about your trainer, but Sherry's engaged, Bridget bought a new horse, Gary is training full-time again, and Amy's mom moved to Arizona and changed her name to Tempe." Good medicine.

Ann and Jim left the next afternoon, and then it was Friday night. On Friday nights when the girls were little, Mickey would put his hands on their heads to bless them. It would be the beginning of the Jewish Sabbath, and we'd light candles and have dinner. After dinner, Mickey would play Hebrew melodies on his accordion, a unique talent for anyone, even a judge. The cat would run and hide under our bed while the girls danced and sang, marching through the living room and into kitchen, sometimes beating a pot with wooden spoons to the rhythm of the songs.

Lani wanted to revive this tradition to celebrate her first Friday night on the veranda. She stood carefully, balancing the heavy cast on her left arm. Mickey blessed our two daughters and then Lani did a barefoot shuffle with Shira while singing in her Darth Vadar whisper. Fortunately for Ward 2B, there was no accordion and no kitchenware.

❏

It appeared that soon we could all return to the States. Lani would still need to be hospitalized, so we had friends in Minneapolis track down the best local facility which turned out to be North Memorial Hospital, just five minutes from our house.

Our social worker, Lorelle, was assigned to work with the insurance company on arranging our flight home and hiring a nurse to accompany us. Since Lani needed to be lying down most of the flight, she and her nurse would fly first class where the seats reclined fully, while the rest of us managed in coach. A date was set, October 21, one month from the accident and many months earlier than we dreamed possible.

The doctors began to get Lani and her records ready for transfer to the States.

One doctor, failing to consider that she was on a heavy dose of blood-thinner, determinedly scraped off the thick scab that formed on her head where the shunt had been. By the time he'd sewn in fresh stitches, she was covered with blood.

Her orthopedic surgeon removed her cast, revealing a four-inch-long scar and a swollen, tender forearm. Her arm wouldn't straighten at the elbow, nor could she turn her wrist from side to side. She would require intensive rehabilitation to regain a functioning left arm and hand.

An ophthalmologist confirmed irreversible loss of vision in her left eye.

An ear doctor assured her that the plane's air pressure wouldn't damage her ears, and hoped the hearing loss from a recently discovered crack in her left eardrum would disappear.

I pushed her to all of the appointments in a wheelchair. It was exhausting and painful for her to sit up because her head was still healing. I thought about how much pain would come from moving an unset broken arm, and then imagined that pain in her head. It must have been excruciating.

"I can't do this, I can't do this," she moaned.

"Yes you can. You're strong," I whispered. And she did. It was the same message my mother had whispered to me almost a month earlier. "Be strong," she said, and now I was passing her torch to my daughter, part of an inheritance to be handed down to the next generation, more precious than a silver teapot or a grandmother's diamond brooch.

After the doctors gave Lani permission to travel home, the rest of our group felt they had permission to do a little traveling of their own. Not very far or for very long, but if Lani were strong enough to tolerate the long flight back to the States, she could handle one day in the hospital without us hovering around her bed. So the next day, everyone went off to see the sights, everyone but me.

There was nothing else I wanted to do, not one thing I wanted to see. When I arrived at the hospital in the morning, Lani's head pain was particularly severe, so she closed her eyes and I held her hand and massaged her fingers. It was quiet, peaceful, just the two of us.

I must have been sitting awkwardly and my back began to ache. The ache spread between my shoulder blades, then traveled down my spine, and connected with the constant tightness in my hip. I didn't dare shift in my chair. If I moved, I'd break the spell, and everything would be hard for Lani again. I stalled until my body would take no more, then shifted slightly. Lani immediately opened her eyes and winced.

Oh, to not have to move. To be grounded in a way that I could hold constantly to my daughter and keep back the pain. How foolish. No mother could do that.

I'm not foolish. I'm scared. And desperate to protect my child. And if that's impossible, I want to comfort her. And if I can't do that, I'm lost.

I was still sitting by her bed when Scott returned from his day trip down the coast, a modern day adventurer with a fresh tan and a new Australian outback hat. When he hugged Lani, I imagined she could smell the rainforest on him. Or the ocean.

Mickey and Shira returned looking gray. They'd seen the accident site near Hervey Bay and visited Emily in the hospital there.

"I was surprised that the car hadn't flipped over going down the hill." Mickey grimaced. "Can you handle looking at photos of the cars?" I didn't know, but I took the pictures. The heavy front end of the oncoming vehicle was totally demolished, and there was appallingly little left of the Falcon that even resembled a car.

"I'm so angry," Shira fumed. "I went to the youth hostel to find the driver of the car, that English girl who lost control of the Falcon. But she wasn't there and no one knew when she'd be back. I wondered if she was there and hiding out in someone's room. I wanted to tear through that whole place. I don't know what I would have said, or done when I found her, but I really wanted to see her. I really wanted to see her." She crumpled into a chair. "Well, she's going to remain faceless. Crap."

Scott shifted the conversation. "So, how's Emily?"

"She seems to be doing her best, just like Lani." Shira was somber.

Mickey said, "I suggested several times that her father transfer her here, where she and Lani can be together, but he wasn't interested."

After Saturday's adventures, we assumed Sunday would be a slow and easy day, so Mickey and Shira slept in. Scott and I walked to the hospital together and were sitting with Lani when a small, gray-haired man in a wrinkled suit walked up and dropped his battered briefcase on Lani's bed. Lani winced from the jarring. Without any introductions or explanation he opened the case, took out a stethoscope, and began to examine her.

Shocked, Scott and I jumped up. "Who are you and what do you think you're doing to my daughter?"

"Stop that right now!" Scott growled protectively.

Small, dull eyes looked at us from a face that was as wrinkled as his suit. "I'm the doctor that was sent by your solicitor, your attorney. I have to perform an independent examination of the patient for your insurance claim." He turned back to Lani and started to poke at her again.

"Stop it right now! I want to see some identification."

He dug into his briefcase and found a business card, and I noticed papers from our attorney scatter on the bed. We'd been told to expect this exam, and it needed to be done before we left, but this man was a travesty. I thought Scott might strangle him with his own stethoscope.

He looked in her eyes. "That left eye is certainly bad. No sight there." He checked her arm. "You're not going to have much use of that arm or hand."

I wanted to scream. He tapped her knee to test her reflexes. What does that have to do with anything? I wanted to drag him out of there by his greasy hair.

"Her medical file is at least three-volumes thick. Have you even read her file? It's clear you haven't read her file. Just stop and look at it." Schmuck!

He grudgingly opened her file, glanced through it. Then he packed up and hurried away without a word. We were furious. Even the nurses in the ward were upset.

I was most enraged with myself. Of course, how predictable. *What is wrong with me? I still can't protect my daughter. What kind of guardian am I? I keep trying, and I keep failing.*

While I wallowed in my familiar black hole, Lani began to cry. It was the first time since the accident I'd seen her cry, and I set my own emotions aside. Even though it seemed too little too late, I complained to our attorney about the incident. Still the nice girl, I was clear and controlled as I explained what had happened.

Damn, my hip hurts!

When Mickey arrived, he suggested I'd feel better if I went with him for a short walk. We went outside and saw Dr. Eustas leaning against the side of the building, having a cigarette. We hadn't seen him since our initial meeting that first night in the ICU, and it was fitting to see him again on this last day and to say goodbye.

"I've been keeping tabs on Lani's progress since that first night. She's a success for us all. She's the miracle that we don't always see in the ICU." He took a last drag on his cigarette, dropped it on the sidewalk, ground it with his foot, and looked up at Mickey. "I'm glad we didn't have to share all that information with your wife."

I looked at Dr. Eustas, confused. "What information? I don't understand."

"That first night your husband asked me not to share everything with you."

He did what!? My mind raced. To cover my humiliation, I forced a smile and tried to make a joke. "Oh, that's okay. There are some things I don't share with him either."

Dr. Eustas smiled back, nodded, and walked away. My smile fell to the ground with the cigarette butts, and I glared at Mickey. "That's the most arrogant, disrespectful thing anyone has ever done to me. Didn't you think the *little woman* could handle it? How dare you? HOW DARE YOU?"

I was trembling. "Did you think I didn't know she might die? Did you think I didn't know the other possibilities? I have been betrayed. You betrayed me." First he deserted me during Lani's life-threatening, six-hour surgery, and now I find that he's lied to me from the beginning of this nightmare. Who is this man? Is he reacting to the pressure of the accident with aberrant behavior or is he being unmasked, is the true Mickey emerging? Oh, God.

"I'm sorry. I wanted to protect you," he offered.

"If that's true, you would never have left me during Lani's first surgery." I turned and walked back into the hospital. I did not ask myself how else he might have deceived me over the years, how many times he was not caught. I could only deal with one life-changing event at a time, and Lani was still priority number one.

She was anxious about returning to the States, leaving the doctors and nurses she trusted. She didn't want to say goodbye to Scott who needed to return to school in Amherst. I was anxious about returning home with a man I no longer trusted. I didn't want to lose the vision of my husband as a fine and honorable man.

The morning before our flight, we brought Lani the clothes she requested to wear the next day and gathered around her bed, fidgeting. Mickey's leg jiggled. I tapped my fingers on the side of my chair. Scott kept getting in and out of his chair. Every time he stood up, Shira sat down. And every time he sat down, Shira stood up. Lani was frowning. "Would you all get out of here? You're making me crazy!" Not subtle, but smart. We scattered.

CHAPTER

Eight

Tuesday, October 20, 1998

On our last night in Brisbane, the owner of the Gregory Terrace treated us to a farewell champagne dinner. After dinner, we packed and went to bed. I lay all night with eyes closed, arms folded across my chest, floating close to sleep but never falling into it. Nothing else was mentioned about the Dr. Eustas episode. Mickey and I acted like it was just another jarring bump in the road, and it added to the jumble in my head and a sinking feeling that something else was broken.

When we arrived at the hospital in the morning, Lani lay on her bed, dressed in torn blue jeans and her Dave Matthews T-shirt, holding her Baubie's blanket. The last time I saw her wear that shirt was the day of her college graduation. Before she changed for the ceremony, we were in the park and she was running to catch one of Mickey's wild Frisbee throws and laughing, her golden future ensured.

A sound beside me announced the arrival of the nurse who would travel with us. I turned to greet a tall, lovely woman who appeared to be in her early thirties. She returned my smile, set down her oversized tote bag that bulged with files, x-rays, and medications, and held out her hand. "Good morning. I'm Cheryl. I will be traveling with you, and as you can probably tell from everything in my tote, I've already been briefed on your daughter's condition." Her handshake was competent and reassuring. "I travel with patients a lot, but I've not been to the States before. I'd love to make a vacation out of it after we get Lani settle in the hospital in Minneapolis, but I have another job coming up right away so I'll have to turn around and fly right back to Australia, though I am hoping to get a few hours at the Mall of America.

People do this all the time. Take their broken children home.

The 2B nurses settled Lani gently into a wheelchair, we said our goodbyes, and began our last walk down the familiar hallway passing the small conference room where we first sat with Dr. D'urso. The door was closed, possibly protecting the next family praying for their miracle. In the waiting room where we spent our first night, a man stared at the TV while a woman sat, eyes closed, with a ragged magazine in her lap.

We stopped one last time at the ICU door and every nurse in the ward came to offer hugs and warm wishes, smiles and tears. Janelle and Amanda were even on duty once again. "Thank you for reminding us why we do the work that we do."

Then it was time to leave for the airport. We made a dramatic exit in a limousine. It was cheaper than an ambulance, we could all fit into it, and there was still room for Lani to lie down if necessary. We must have looked like an odd little touring company climbing into our limo: Scott the leading man in his wide-brimmed Australian hat; Lani, the fragile leading lady; Shira and I supporting actresses; Cheryl the props person with her loaded bags; and Mickey, the director, telling everyone where to sit.

In high spirits, Lani sat up, and at a stoplight she tested the limo's privacy tinted glass window by grinning and sending a very unladylike hand gesture to the people in the car next to us. When we arrived at the airport, a wheelchair was waiting for

Lani, but no one could find our reservations. Cheryl wheeled Lani to rest near the departure gate, while Scott and Shira used a luggage cart to push each other back and forth across the ticketing area running as fast as they could. I didn't intend to tell them it wasn't appropriate or that they needed to stop. I only wished I could release my stress as easily.

Finally, with our reservations sorted out, we joined Cheryl and Lani at the end of a long concourse to wait for our flight. Scott sat down on a blue cushioned bench and Lani lay next to him, resting her head on his lap. They were beginning their goodbyes. He would leave us in Los Angeles where he boarded his flight home to Massachusetts. Shira walked off to find a genuine chocolate malt for Lani that would make up for all the fraudulent thick chocolate powdered drinks she'd swallowed in the past two weeks.

Mickey and I strolled off idly and in a moment of determination, I spoke up. "Mickey, we have to clear something up before we get on the plane."

"What?" He looked confused.

"Do you have any idea how controlling you have been, what a bully you have been this past month? It might be the stress, but you can't bring that behavior back to the States."

"Was I? I had no idea." He looked surprised. "I'm sorry. I apologize. I really do. Do you think I should apologize to Shira, too?"

I nodded and he went off to find Shira. I was relieved I had spoken up. Finally. It was simple, just not easy. And once again, he said he was sorry. It sounds good when he says it, but I couldn't help but wonder if it meant anything. Did I really think he would drop a piece of his personality in the Brisbane airport like a disposable cup of cold coffee. But I confidently boarded the plane taking us from Brisbane to Sydney. When the flight attendant found out about Lani's accident, he put a bottle of wine in my purse and winked at me saying, "You're going to need this." And when we reached Sydney we received a little cheer from the Qantas representative escorting us to our connecting flight. "You seem like a wonderful family."

She saw Shira and Lani exchange a look and roll their eyes, and she smiled. "Things aren't suppose to be perfect here on Earth; perfection is for paradise."

Thank you, dear lady.

During the flight to Los Angeles I was able to eat, sleep, and even watch one of the movies. Mickey surprised me with a gift of earrings and a matching bracelet from the duty-free catalogue that I assumed celebrated that we were going home, apologized for his behavior, and affirmed he loved me.

I love you too, Mickey. In spite of everything.

Do I?

I kissed him on the cheek, curled up in my seat, and covered myself with the small, blue blanket from the plane.

When we reached Los Angeles, a mustached, toothless attendant got us through customs quickly then led us to a bus that would take us to the terminal where we could collect our baggage. The bus wasn't handicapped accessible, but undeterred, he tried to tip the wheelchair and flip it onto the bus with Lani still in it. Scott came to the rescue, helping Lani stand and climb onto the bus while our guide followed, banging the empty chair up the bus steps and through the aisle. When we reached the baggage claim area, Lani was reunited with her chair, and our ground attendant stayed with her while the rest of us raced to the luggage carousel.

Suddenly, the attendant was next to us trying to be helpful.

Oh my God, where is Lani?

He'd left her alone and unprotected in the middle of the airport chaos. I found her curled in her chair with tears in her eyes. While she was still feeling vulnerable, Scott had to hurry to another gate for his flight to Boston. She didn't want to say goodbye to him like an invalid, so she put both feet carefully on the ground, placed her good hand on the armrest of the wheelchair, and pushed slowly until she was standing, facing him. They hugged, a tender, tearful hug, and then he was gone.

We were escorted to a van that took us to the Northwest Airlines terminal, a dirty, crowded building where noisy, pushy travelers swarmed the ticket counters, and the blast of flight announcements could hardly be heard. It looked like it would take a long time to get our boarding passes. I was tired and Lani looked exhausted, so I stepped to the counter, admittedly ahead of another waiting traveler, looked at the ticket agent, and begged in the kindest, most reasonable voice possible, "My daughter is very sick. Can you please help us?"

Face tight, she looked up impatiently. "Well? Is she too sick to fly?"

"Uh. Nooo?"

"So wait your turn," she snapped.

Defeated, I nodded to the top of her head and went back to my family.

Our flight didn't leave for two hours, and after we finally got our tickets, Lani needed to lie down. All we saw were rows of individual chairs strung together like mutant pearls, so we sought out the Northwest World Perks Club on the second floor and walked in. The door shut silently behind us, and suddenly it was quiet; only muted conversation, the rustle of a newspaper, a TV murmur. And there were soft chairs and sofas. Heaven.

The young, stylish receptionist greeted us quietly and said Lani and Cheryl could use the facility, because they had first class tickets, but the rest of us had to leave. She was sorry. Policy.

"My family has to stay with me." Lani sobbed from her wheelchair. "I almost died. I'm not leaving my family. They have to stay with me."

"I know you have rules," I said to the receptionist, "but you need to make an exception." I was determined to take a stand even though I had failed miserably at the ticket counter. "My daughter did almost die. She's still recovering. She's very weak and feeling extremely vulnerable and we're going to stay here with her. Thank you for understanding."

Before the receptionist could respond, we moved past her into the room. Honestly, I didn't care if she understood or not, but she said nothing further. I gave her a heartfelt smile and "thank you" when, ninety minutes later, our refreshed family left the room.

The Minneapolis flight was leaving first and Shira had to wait another hour before she could return to Albuquerque. It was so hard to say goodbye to her. I didn't want her out of my sight. I kept turning around to wave goodbye as we walked down the jet way to the plane. Then her face was gone. I found my seat, buckled in, and put my head in my hand. Almost home and airborne on this last leg of our long journey, I looked up to see Lani, with Cheryl at her side, walking carefully, slowly, back from first class to visit us.

❑

Arriving in Minneapolis at 10:30 at night, weary to the bone, and the last four people on the plane, we waited ten minutes for an attendant to bring a wheelchair. Lani settled into it, we picked up our carry-on luggage, and hauled our exhausted bodies down the jet way to the gate area. And there our family stood, wearing smiles and carrying balloons. Mickey's brother Harley, Lani's cousins, my parents. Louie and Terry were even in town from Boston.

"Welcome home!"

"How was your flight?"

"We're so glad you're here!"

"Give me a hug!"

"So wonderful to see you!"

"You must be exhausted!"

Our physical and emotional load became lighter with each hug and kiss. I watched each person approach Lani and swiftly mask their shock and blink away tears and I saw her through their eyes; hunched in her wheelchair, thirty pounds thinner, a shaved section of her head covered with a bandage and surrounded by new sprouts of hair; a blue iris nestled in the right corner of her left eye, staring unseeing at the side of her nose; a trach scar, still thick and raw; a left arm lying thin and immobile. Only her smile was recognizable.

Thinking about how she looked made me conscious of my own appearance. Rumpled and frumpy, no makeup and drooping with exhaustion, I reached up to fluff my matted hair. Aware of the futility of my gesture, I was embarrassed to have revealed my vanity. I cared nothing about my appearance in Australia. Why would it matter now, when I was surrounded by family? But family can be more dangerous than strangers. I felt my family had certain expectations of me, and the expectations were not only to act my part, but to look my part.

Get a grip, Barb. Look at these people. They're thrilled to see us, and they're not judging you. They're not even looking at you; they're looking at Lani.

The judging would come later, I was certain. "Poor girl, she's letting herself go. What happened to her? She was such a lovely lady. Have you seen her lately? So sad."

It was sad. More than anyone knew. I'd let myself go long before the accident. I'd let go of my genuine self, piece by piece over the years. The right lipstick and a good hair cut were just part of my camouflage. Luckily, no one noticed the exposed me. The welcoming committee escorted us through the terminal to a limo waiting to take us to the hospital where Cheryl delivered her tote full of medical files and x-rays, and where Lani was wheeled into a private carpeted room with her own bathroom and shower and phone and TV and VCR.

Although it was after midnight by the time she got settled, Lani was energized and sat in bed, her Baubie's blanket beside her, detailing the specifics of her condition to three nurses. Mickey and I interrupted her for a moment to kiss her good-night, and then we joined Cheryl in the back of the limo for the short ride to our familiar driveway. As we unlocked our garage door, the driver brought our luggage in and then left to take Cheryl to a hotel near the airport for a few hours of sleep before her return trip.

We were home. Our house had stood solidly waiting for us all this time. The thirty-year-old sofa from my aunt, the wooden coffee table from a garage sale, the lamp from my folks' basement, were all in their cozy grouping. The living room curtains still needed cleaning, the hardwood floor was still worn in the same pattern, and the outdated orange kitchen counter tops still glowed. Our girls loved this kitchen and were confident that orange counters were bound to come back into fashion very soon.

In the kitchen, there were balloons tied to boxes of macaroni and cheese, my favorite. The refrigerator was stocked with casseroles, garlic mashed potatoes, an entire cooked turkey and a pot of healing chicken soup. Confused at our sudden return, our cat kept talking to us. He wouldn't let me pick him up, so I sat on the floor while he rubbed against my leg. I felt the weight of him, the warmth of him, his softness holding me as dearly as if he were wrapping arms around me.

I went upstairs to shower. Our small, white-tiled bathroom seemed elegant. I used a fragranced cleansing gel and dried off with a fluffy blue towel. I went into our bedroom where pictures of our daughters hung on the wall, my grandfather's rocking chair sat in a corner, and a partially read book lay on my night table. With a grateful sigh, I lay down on my own bed and closed my eyes.

I felt comforted that nothing had changed, though indeed I knew everything had. A month ago, in an instant, our world cracked. Would the foundation hold? I had no idea and, for the moment, it was enough to let the familiar settle around me like my quilt, safe and warm.

I waited for sleep. My hip ached. My mind raced. It was pointless. With a sigh I sat up and looked at the bedroom door. I shuffled to the closet, found my gray bathrobe with Tinkerbell on the pocket, a gift from Shira. I shrugged it on and went downstairs, sorted a month's worth of mail with Mickey, and did three loads of laundry. At 8:30 A.M. I put on a clean shirt and a fresh pair of jeans and drove back to the hospital with Mickey for a 9:00 A.M. meeting in Lani's hospital room with her new neurologist.

❏

Friday, October 23, 1998

Dr. Brodsky, natty in his sport coat and tie, greeted us with a handshake and a warm smile. "I've studied the x-rays you brought from Brisbane. The Australian medical team obviously was exceptionally skilled because this truly is a miracle."

He looked at Lani. "I want you to begin your therapy today. Do you feel strong enough?"

Lani nodded, right eye intensely focused.

"Okay. This is how we'll proceed. You'll have three therapy sessions every morning: speech therapy, physical therapy, and occupational therapy. Then you'll have lunch, a little rest, and repeat the same three in the afternoon."

Lani nodded again. Dr. Brodsky shook her right hand, completing their contract, wished us well, and continued on his rounds. I felt green from exhaustion, so we kissed Lani goodbye and went home. I walked in the door, up the stairs, fell on the bed, and was asleep before I could pull the quilt above my knees.

Lani maintained her rigorous schedule without complaint. The physical therapists worked to help her regain her balance and strength. She had to overcome her lessened depth perception from loss of sight in one eye. A therapist assisted her as she walked on a low narrow board, putting one foot in front of the other.

Another therapist stood beside her as she climbed up and down a set of five steps. It was simple, but not easy. Not easy at all.

Occupational therapists worked with her arm. It was bent at the elbow and held there by muscles that had shortened and atrophied from being immobilized for so long. Her wrist wouldn't rotate, so she was also not able to turn her hand from side to side. The therapists worked gently and patiently to stretch her muscles, careful to protect her tender, swollen incision. An x-ray showed extra bone growing in her elbow joint that could, if not stopped, block movement permanently. Determined, Lani raced against the growing bone, taking medication to retard bone growth, and working alone at night lying in her bed, pushing on her arm. Progress was painful and measured in millimeters.

Healing her vocal chords was just as slow, but not as painful. She could still speak only in her Darth Vadar whisper. Her speech therapists had Lani sing a note, any note, for as long as she could. Even if it was a whisper. Off key was fine. Her voice lasted six seconds. An average person she was told, can hold a note for twenty seconds, so she was to practice every day, stretching to another second.

She was given more standardized intelligence tests, searching for indications of brain damage. There were puzzles and word games and more exercises. She completed every test successfully and usually in record time.

Her mind was whole and her spirit was strong, but her body was weak and her schedule intense. Eating a meal was its own unique workout. She concentrated on chewing carefully and swallowing deliberately. It was such a slow process that, after lunch, she never had time to rest before her next set of therapies began.

When Lani first began these therapies, an aid helped her into a wheelchair and wheeled her to her appointments. After a few days, however, she got herself into the chair, pushed the footrests out of the way, and walked the chair to therapy. By the end of the week, when she abandoned her wheelchair, carried her charts, and walked to therapy, the staff determined she was ready for her re-entry process to begin.

The first exercise was a short field trip to a shopping mall. She joined a shy teenager who had overdosed on drugs and jumped out a window, fracturing his skull, and a beautiful African woman in her sixties who spoke no English and was recovering from a stroke. An interesting trio. True to form and despite her handicap, Lani found a great skirt on sale.

The day after the field trip, she had a violent episode of vertigo, losing all sense of up, down, and where she was. It was unclear if this was a result of fatigue or a reaction to a change in medication. An MRI was ordered and something suspicious appeared on the film. I wasn't at the hospital when Lani was given these results, so when she called me sobbing and terrified, I peeled out of my driveway in my red Grand Am and didn't stop until I screeched into a parking space in the hospital lot. The elevator to the fourth floor was slow, but I made up time racing down the hallway, skidding to a stop outside her room. There she sat, calm and composed, next to a nurse who was holding her hand.

I'm getting too old for this.

Another MRI the next day revealed that the suspicious shape had been a shadow. Lani was fine. I was fading.

She had conquered the mall. Next challenge, the kitchen. Not exactly familiar territory for Lani. This would be interesting. The occupational therapy kitchen was used to teach patients to be self-sufficient once again. Since chocolate chip cookies and peanut butter and jelly sandwiches were her full repertoire, the nurses decided that making cookies would be great therapy for everyone.

On Friday, she mixed the cookie batter and refrigerated it. On Saturday morning, she was to bake the cookies. Then Saturday afternoon she'd come home for a one-night trial run. My mother came with me to the hospital to keep Lani company in the kitchen until it was time to bring her home.

Mickey was not available. He had returned to work after our first week back in the States and liked to spend Saturdays in his office catching up on paperwork. My mother and I watched as Lani confidently scooped great careless globs of batter onto the cookie sheets.

"Now Lani," the therapist chided, "look at what you're doing. Don't you think you're doing this a little too quickly? And you're putting so much cookie dough in each mound? Don't you think that's a little too much? The cookies will be sooo big!"

Lani glared and then blew up. "I'm in a hurry because I want to go home. And I always scoop large mounds of dough onto the sheet. I like big cookies! You should have read my chart. There is nothing wrong with my mind. There's nothing wrong with my skills. There's nothing wrong with me!"

Her speech therapist would have been awed by the sheer volume of her voice. The occupational therapist was shocked. My mother was embarrassed. I was silently rooting for Lani.

You go, girl. Maybe I can learn to do that.

The cookies were big and delicious. Lani piled them on a plate and brought them to her nurses. Then we packed her up and brought her home for the night.

She laid on the sofa and watched TV, then sat in the kitchen and had a peanut butter and jelly sandwich. It was an exquisitely ordinary time. That night, I tucked her into bed in her own room, with horse show ribbons hanging on the wall above pictures of her jumping her big, gray mare. Propped up with pillows and covered with blankets, she looked at me. "It's so strange, Mom, but I thought a lot about death before leaving on this trip. There was no reason to, except maybe because I was going to be gone for so long. I knew I'd had a wonderful life and done so many things and had amazing experiences and great friends. My life has already been so full. I knew there'd be nothing to regret." She closed her eyes briefly. "But I decided I wasn't ready to die yet, especially because of Scott. I wanted to find out what would happen with Scott."

She had decided to live before she ever went on the trip. I kissed her good night and we both whispered, "Sweet dreams." I closed her door quietly and closed my eyes. She was home.

Sunday, we woke to sunshine and temperatures in the sixties, unusually warm weather for the end of October in Minnesota. After a lazy morning and a breakfast request for her dad's pancakes, I bundled her in a jacket, scarf, and gloves. We walked slowly to the park at the end of the block and we sat for almost two hours on the grass under a large elm. She talked mainly about Scott; how they met, what they did during their summer in Boston. "I hope you don't mind that I'm running up a large long distance phone bill from North Memorial. I'm calling Scott a lot. I can't help it." She turned to look at me, to test my expression.

"No, I don't mind at all. It's wonderful." I laughed.

I got tired before she did, and we walked back to the house where we found three of her elementary school friends waiting to cheer her up. Judd hadn't taken any chances with his mission to bring cheer and came dressed as a chicken. His Halloween costume, I assumed. I hoped.

It was getting close to suppertime, so I made pasta and salad for everyone. Then my body told me I'd pushed too far, and I excused myself and went upstairs to lie down.

Stop pretending this is a normal Sunday night dinner, and that you don't ache because Lani has to go back to the hospital tonight, and that, as grateful as you are, the pain isn't unbearable.

Two days later, Lani was permanently released from the hospital and sent home with pills for the pain in her head, pills to retard bone growth in her elbow joint, and pills to thin her blood and reduce the chance of a stroke until her right carotid artery healed. In preparation, I stocked up on groceries. Joey, Sharon, and Cathleen, the cashiers behind the service counter, greeted me with hugs and smiles, and required a full update. At the drug store, I bought a stool for Lani to sit on in the shower, and a few other items that seemed more appropriate for aging parents, than a twenty-two-year-old daughter.

Our house, like her hospital room, began to fill with cards and gifts. One of the gifts was a healing bracelet of small stones and amulets that was made especially for her. The designer said she'd had a strong sense that Lani was a powerful young woman. She warned that it was common to lose the bracelet after one healed, and after a few months that was exactly what happened. I loved the idea of a healing bracelet and asked her to design one for me. I wore it constantly, and although it fell off twice, I didn't lose it. I felt I was being told, "Keep this, kiddo; you're going to need this for a while."

Our daily routine was simple. Lani awoke, took a pain pill, and waited thirty minutes for it to take effect before she could manage to move out of bed. Then with one hand on the wall to steady herself, she went into the bathroom and sat in the tub to take her shower. Then it was back to bed where I rubbed a thick lotion onto her dry legs and feet. Finally, we made the slow trip to the family room sofa, where I brought her breakfast, and we watched TV and talked.

One morning after four pieces of French toast, she lay with her feet in my lap and asked, "Mom, did I tell you about the two crazy dreams I had while I was in my coma?"

"No, tell me." I began massaging her left foot.

"In the first dream, people were leaving, going someplace, and I was supposed to go with them, but I decided not to. I wanted to stay."

"Oh Lani, I don't think that was a dream at all. I think that was when you made your decision to stay. And you know, you're pretty stubborn once you make up your mind about something!"

"Mmmm, that could be, Mom. But how about my other dream? That was all about Muppets in our backyard, and visions of evolution, and more Muppets. That one was pretty strange."

I chuckled. "I'm guessing that dream was brought on by the heavy dose of barbiturates they gave you when you started coming out of the coma. When your brain activity increased, so did the swelling. So to keep your brain swelling down, the doctors put you in an artificial coma with the drugs. And drugs can give you some strange dreams."

"Drug-induced dreams. Sounds like some people's entire college experience." She laughed.

I began to massage her other foot. "Usually, I can't remember my dreams, but I had a really vivid one last night. Can I tell you mine?"

"Sure."

"You brought a horse into the family room and gave it to me. I was sitting right here and you led this horse through those doors and handed me the reins."

"Mom, you're getting weirder than you used to be. You need more rest."

"Probably, but you know how I loved Tattoo."

"Yep."

"Well, I think you were bringing back to me a part of myself that I love and that was missing. A vital part of myself."

"What do you think that part is?"

I shrugged. I couldn't remember. I'd been separated from it for too long. After a few moments of silence, Lani picked up the remote and turned on the TV. I finished rubbing her feet and covered them with the afghan and closed my eyes.

I liked my interpretation of the dream, but I didn't feel full and vital, only empty and drained, and I was beginning to be curious about what the future would hold, not just for my daughter, but for me as well. I still felt the loss of Tattoo, the pain of giving up something I loved and that gave me such joy, filling a place so deep at my core. A pain I had learned I could ignore if I stayed busy enough with my Mary Kay business and the details of life.

Now, in a dream, I was offered myself again; it left an ache in my body. I felt the emptiness I'd done my best to ignore. It was so heavy. How can something empty be so heavy? Had I been betrayed or had I betrayed myself? I shifted away from the question, adjusting myself on the sofa, and I felt the ache in my hip, still with me from Australia.

Ache or not, I had Lani to care for. I stayed busy cooking meals for my constantly hungry daughter. When she wasn't eating, she was on the phone with Scott, or asleep under layers of blankets.

Sometimes she raged against her illness. "I'm twenty-two years old and the first thing I do when I wake up is take a pain pill and I still can't move, the pain is so bad. I can't stand it."

I was grateful she could vent her feelings, so I just sat with her and listened without comment.

But, one day, she aimed her rage at me with an intensity that took my breath away. A technician had just brought a brace that fit over her elbow and forearm and could be adjusted to stretch her arm muscles, gradually increasing her range of motion. "You need to wear this brace thirty minutes, twice a day," the fragile-looking young man advised. "And remember to increase the angle just a little each time you wear it." He adjusted the device cautiously and Lani grimaced in pain.

"Don't push too hard, Lani," I said.

"*Shut up!*" She screamed at me, her face red and contorted.

I recoiled. Her words hit me like a fist. Hurt and humiliated, I excused myself and left the room.

The technician feigned ignorance. After he left for his next appointment, she found me in my bedroom and apologized. "I'm sorry, Mom, but you can't ask if something is too hard or if I'm too tired. That's negative talk and I can't hear anything negative now."

That's a mom's job. Isn't that what moms are supposed to say? I'm just doing my job. I don't know how else to do this.

CHAPTER

Nine

I was desperate for some healing of my own, so Mickey and I started going out to early dinners with friends. One evening, in a little Greek restaurant, a woman commented about the importance of a positive attitude. "It's amazing what a positive attitude can do. Whenever I go shopping, I visualize exactly what I need, and it makes everything so much easier."

You must have overdosed on self-help books, honey. How can you equate shopping with Lani's accident? Do you not get what is going on here?

Sitting in the booth of a burger joint, a woman pawed at my arm, sighing, "You poor thing, how terrible, you poor thing, how terrible."

Back off, lady. I will not be treated like a victim!

How easily empathy gets lost in translation when it's more about the giver than the receiver. I saw what the experience that first month could have been if we'd been in the States. I imagined visits from the moaners. "Oye, this breaks my heart. Oye, it's so terrible. How can you stand it? It's too much. It's just too much."

Then there would have been the promoters of positive thinking commenting about our family's challenge. *Challenge*. Now
there's a manipulative word that reduces pain and terror to a
formula, denies its dark reality, and diminishes the courage it
took to survive. But I'm most distressed to recognize that I've
used both of those scripts, and maybe worse, because I hadn't
yet stood in the darkness.

Now that I had, I was writing new scripts. When asked how
Lani was doing, I answered, "Great!" When asked if she had
any residual affects, I answered, "Hardly any." When they said
it must have been hard, I answered, "Yes, it was very hard. And
how is your family?" I wasn't ready to tell my story. I wouldn't
dishonor a sacred experience by sharing it casually over a
Caesar salad.

Friends commented that they couldn't believe I handled everything so well, that I stayed so strong. Usually it was a compli-
ment, but every once in awhile there was an implication that
they'd noticed my quietness and judged me as weak. My husband is loud, and people see him as more. I am quiet, and people see me as less. I'm not. I'm simply quiet.

I was introduced to a man whose teenage son had died in a car
accident just a few years earlier, who said, "Everything happens
for a reason." Startled, I stared at him, and even as my heart
went out to this father, I controlled the impulse I had to smack
him as hard as I could.

No one could stare at a comatose daughter for ten days and
justify her condition by saying, "Everything happens for a reason." Maybe this man had been screaming *"Why?"* for so long
that he was exhausted and this was the only answer he could
find that would take the pain away, or give him the strength to
live with his pain. Was this faith? Or was this the only option
left that allowed him to go on with his life? Maybe that's what
faith is.

Because Lani came back to us, it would be easy for me to say
that everything happens for a reason. How convenient. I
wouldn't have to question. It would give order to my world, like

going through life with a golden key. But then I remember the teenage boys from 2B and I choose to believe that when things happen, we can decide to find a reason; to learn, to help others, to create a blessing somehow. It's not that I have no faith. I have tremendous faith. But going through life without a magic key feels more honest. Too much is mystery.

❏

Saturday, November 12, 1998

I was on red alert. Lani was driving to the airport alone at night to pick up three friends from college who were coming to visit for the weekend. I sat on the sofa and worried about how she would handle the traffic and the parking and the crowds. She came home smiling and light. I was exhausted.

When her girlfriends followed her through the door, juggling their backpacks and laughing, the energy level in our house surged. They were beams of sunlight burning away the fog that had hung heavy in the air. They were cold beer on a hot day or an "I Love Lucy" rerun after a depressing documentary. They watched videos, ordered pizzas, and solved the problems of the world. Their laughter and vitality scattered in the bedrooms like discarded T-shirts, filled the kitchen like the dirty dishes and empty pizza cartons, and gusted through the family room like fresh air through the patio door on a windy day.

Two days after they left, Shira flew into Minneapolis for Thanksgiving. That Friday night, we three Greenberg girls lit the Sabbath candles. Though we cried, our tears did not dissolve the laughter left by Lani's friends. We were a full-service home. Laughter and tears. We had it all.

The day after Shira left, Patrick arrived from Boston, tall, charming, with dark hair and mischievous smile. He was recovering well from the accident, though he still had more surgeries ahead of him. It was important for Lani and Patrick to be able to talk together about the accident, to sort out emotions, to make sense of life after senselessly being so close to death.

I had an opportunity to have my own conversations with him. One day while we sat talking in the kitchen, he showed me his scars from the accident. And then his scars from football. And then his scars from hockey. *Boys!*

In mid-December, two weeks after Patrick left, Mickey, Lani, and I flew to Albuquerque to see Shira's dance company perform their second annual "Nutcracker on the Rocks." Saturday morning, after Friday's successful opening night, Shira was busy at the studio, so the three of us drove to the mountain range east of the city where Lani pointed to a massive outcropping of rocks and announced, "I'm going to climb that."

I was stunned, but I knew by then to keep my mouth shut.

"It only looks big," she said as she turned her back to us and began. Frail, with one good eye and one good arm, she didn't hesitate. Mickey and I couldn't keep up. I sat on a boulder and watched her determined march. She climbed what we couldn't, as it should have been. This was her journey, not ours. After twenty minutes, she stood with arms outstretched, triumphant at the top of the ridge.

I looked at her, tiny against the boundless sky. She was rushing boldly back into the world, believing fully in the unlimited possibilities life still held for her. *What possibilities are mine?*

We were almost back to our car, on the flat ground, when my feet got tangled with each other and I fell, landing on my butt with a thud. Mickey and I laughed, and Lani looked at me and shook her head. I didn't know then that soon, when the obstacles were cleared from my path, I would fall again and fall hard.

❑

Lani was on the move, and there was no stopping her. Scott's mother invited her to Boston as a Christmas surprise for her son, reassuring me that as a former ICU nurse, she would watch Lani closely, and it would be a safe way for Lani to practice being away from home on her own. I agreed and hoped it would be good practice for me in letting go. Not that I had much choice.

Lani wanted to make the surprise one that Scott would remember, so she appeared on his doorstep in Boston wearing a Santa outfit. The surprise and the trip were a success, and Scott returned with Lani to spend a week in Minneapolis with us. It was wonderful to see them together; relaxed, in love, sitting on the sofa styling each other's hair, picking food off each other's plates, holding hands in front of the open refrigerator, looking for snacks.

Separation was not an option, so when Scott went back to Amherst in January for his last semester of classes, Lani went, too. She got a job at the university as an assistant coach to the women's crew team.

She was moving too fast for me. I couldn't keep up. She was going back out into the world, a dangerous, uncertain place, and I was so tired of being afraid. There had to be another emotion to feel. I wanted to slap myself upside the head, *"Just knock it off, Barb. Handle it. Lani is. She's back in Massachusetts. Mickey's handling it. He went back to work almost immediately after we returned home. Just get a grip."* I couldn't convince myself.

❏

School was an emotional roller coaster for Lani, and she called home often. She loved the graduate class she was taking. She hated her job. She was living with Scott and loved it when he fixed her dinner. She hated being so weak that she had to spend all her free time sleeping. Some calls were painfully sad. "I'm home alone, lying in bed in the dark. Please tell me a story." Some calls were filled with violent outbursts. "Why am

I alive if all I am doing is sitting here?" She was terribly frustrated, feeling that her life was on hold, but sometimes sitting is the wisest thing to do. She had plowed through her therapies and attacked the mountain in Albuquerque. Now she had come to a place where she needed to be still and gentle with herself.

"Lani, you have always been a very strong woman, and when you get through to the other side of this, you will be a very wise woman," I offered, trying just to listen without giving advice. She was angry when I gave it, and she was angry when I didn't. She must have hated feeling dependent on me when all she wanted was to be her own person. So I became her emotional punching bag. I couldn't win and I couldn't get out of the way and she knew I would never strike back. I remember hanging up the phone after one of her calls and going downstairs to change the laundry, still my connection to normal. I didn't make it to the washing machine before I had to sit down on the floor and sob. *I'm so tired of this.*

But life stumbled forward. In March, Lani made her speech at the crew team banquet. It was the speech she had composed in her head while lying in her hospital bed in 2B. Four hundred people gave her a standing ovation. She sent us pictures. She was in a long black dress, holding a bouquet of flowers, standing with Scott. She looked like a beautiful, strong woman, a warrior goddess victorious, her inner turmoil undetected.

In April, she flew home for the Passover holiday. Shira drove in from Albuquerque, and Louie and Terry even returned to Minneapolis. We celebrated with family and a huge dinner: chicken soup for the traditional guests, vegetable soup for the vegetarian, salads, brisket, more veggies, lots of potatoes and stacks of matzah. Mickey began the evening by blessing his girls. He placed his hands on their heads and haltingly, with tears, repeated the same blessing he had given Lani before her trip.

We took a lot of pictures that night and got some very interesting results. There was a picture of Lani near the dining room table, bending over just enough, so that her head was behind the light fixture that was hanging from the ceiling and superimposed in such a way that it looked like she was wearing the crown of a warrior goddess. Another photo was of our entire family in front of the fireplace. On the wall behind us was a picture, and the yellow in the picture framed Louie's head. An angel. On the fireplace mantel was a small ceramic sculpture of two birds that had belonged to my grandfather. When the picture was taken, there was a space where someone else could have been standing, and in that space were the birds. My grandfather had joined us in the picture. To keep all of this in perspective, there was a photo of Mickey sitting at the table with a bottle of wine in front of him looking as if he had a cork in his nose. What can I say? Messages from The Beyond or bad camera work?

I should have paid more attention to that last photo.

❑

Lani had five doctors' appointments in the following days and five good reports. Her first appointment was for an MRI to check her right carotid artery. Since it was a nice day, she jogged to and from the hospital. The artery was healed. The neurologist said there should be no more chance of a stroke, and she could wean herself off the blood-thinner. The orthopedist was amazed by the range of motion in her arm and told her she should become an occupational therapist, and she said that was her plan. The ophthalmologist said although there was no sight in her left eye, it was no longer turned inward and no one could tell by looking at her that the eye wasn't normal. And no, she couldn't fix him up with her sister because he was already married. When she returned from her last appointment, I was doing paperwork in the family room.

"The doctors say I'm fine."

"That's so wonderful, Lani. A clean bill of health."

"Clean, but I will never see out of my left eye!"

She left the room. I stared after her. What can I say? She doesn't want a hug. She doesn't want sympathy. The room was empty and cold, and I stared at my papers.

The next day, Lani flew back to school, and Shira got ready for her drive to Albuquerque. We hugged and kissed goodbye in the driveway, she got in her car, and Mickey and I went back into the house. I was sitting on the sofa when the garage door opened, and I heard Shira crying.

"I don't know what's wrong. I don't want to leave. I'm afraid terrible things might happen after I drive away."

I rocked her in my arms and understood. Nothing feels safe anymore. We don't know what actions will result in disaster. Leave? Stay? Which wrong choice will trip the trigger? Which wrong step will set off the avalanche? How will we be able to return to life? Not just skim the surface, but participate in the world again.

Shira had been the first to take that step when she separated from us at the Los Angeles airport, flying back to Albuquerque and plunging back into the pressure of her business: teaching dance classes, holding rehearsals, writing grants, putting out newsletters. She called home often to be reassured that crying for long periods of time for no apparent reason was normal. How could it be any other way? Her grief was as powerful a presence as the mountains at the edge of the city, some days remaining on the periphery of her vision, some days filling the horizon so completely that nothing else was visible.

Lani charged at those mountains, those massive purple boulders—scrambling over anger and frustration, pulling herself across chasms of overwhelming sadness, determined to overcome obstacles she insisted only looked big. But they were big. They were monstrous, and she kept climbing, and I had no doubt she would somehow reach the summit and look down to survey all she had accomplished.

In contrast to his daughters, Mickey seemed confident his climb was over, certain he had done all his necessary grieving in

Australia. He was comfortable back at work, once again in control of the scenery, not interested in rugged terrain or landscapes that took strength and courage to confront.

I could find no familiar landmarks to guide me through this uncharted territory until a friend offered me the opportunity to ride her horse twice a week. The horse was at the same barn I had stabled Tattoo almost fifteen years ago, resting in the same stall. Though he had a fancy show name, everyone called him T. A large, black horse, over seventeen hands, and very gentle, he felt it was his job to keep peace in the pasture. I was told that when a young horse tried to bully a shy mare, T simply grabbed the troublemaker's neck in his strong mouth, picked him up, faced him the other direction, and that was the end of that. And in the barn, if T weren't getting enough attention, he stuck his head out of his stall door and shook sleigh bells hanging nearby until someone came over to pet him and tell him how handsome he was.

I hoped that this chance to ride had reappeared to save me as it did in my dream, but I stopped going to the barn after two months. Even this most powerful medicine couldn't keep me from the approaching darkness. Tears came more often now and at odd times: while driving home from the grocery store, making the bed, washing dishes.

I'd assumed that once things got closer to normal, as they were, I would have a classic come-apart that included not just tears, but screaming, sobbing, and cursing. But instead of exploding outward, I was silently collapsing into myself emotionally and physically. My posture had never been the best, and now I couldn't straighten up at all. Soon, I was curling up daily on the sofa for naps. It didn't feel ominous; it felt safe, like climbing into a lifeboat every afternoon.

Why did I need a lifeboat? What was sinking? I looked around. I was. I sat on the sofa and stared at a tree outside the patio door as though I were staring at a receding shore. It wasn't a pretty tree. It was small, bent awkwardly from the weight of heavy winter snows, with thin branches and few leaves. But neighborhood birds always came to sit and visit, flying off briefly only when the squirrels chased each other across a fragile limb. A tide seemed to be carrying me away from all these signs of life. I rolled between waves of joy and grief, gratitude and terror, relief and fear. Like a castaway on the cold seas, I soon became numb.

The only intense emotion I felt was an occasional flicker of rage at Lani's horse trainer for the hurt she caused my daughter. I knew I should let go of my anger, but I wasn't ready. It was the only thing I could feel, and I held on to it for dear life.

"Release your anger," said proper me.

"Hang on to it, revel in it. Get up close and personal. Scream at her," demanded honest me. "How about slapping her face? Better yet, give her a good punch in the gut."

"You don't really want to cause her pain," said proper me.

"The hell I don't! But if I can't, how about some guilt?"

"Tsk, tsk, you don't want to do that."

"You're right. It's too subtle. I'll just smack her."

I enjoyed my debate as long as I pictured her as a selfish, cold woman. But one day in my imagination, I saw only a frightened, lonely person, isolated in pain of her own making, who had been as good to Lani as she knew how to be. I felt no sympathy for this invention, but she wasn't the focus of my rage any longer. What would happen if I saw her one day at a horse show? Probably nothing. Is that okay? Not yet, but it will be.

Most days I had no energy for rage or for much of anything. I functioned until early afternoon and then retreated to the safety of the sofa where I wedged myself as far as possible into its soft corner. I felt nauseous when I ate. I felt dizzy when I didn't eat. My hip still hurt. I felt like crying all the time, but I couldn't cry enough. I had constant headaches that sparkled behind my eyes. I couldn't make decisions because I was terrified of making mistakes. Mistakes weren't acceptable and were more dangerous than ever. If I didn't do just the right thing, there would be horrible consequences. If the phone rang, I jumped. If Mickey picked it up and didn't respond immediately, I panicked.

I made an appointment with the soft-spoken psychologist who had counseled us briefly when we first returned to the States. She confirmed that I had classic signs of depression. She didn't recommend medication, but she insisted I continue sitting on the sofa as much as possible. It was time for me to heal.

At first, I was grateful that there was a name for what was happening to me. I thought a label would make the process more manageable. My relief was swiftly followed by familiar fear. "You're depressed," a voice sneered, as long bony fingers picked me up and dropped me off the side of a miles-deep canyon. No bottom. Nothingness. My arms and legs flailing. Nothing to grab hold of to stop my fall. I can't be depressed. It means I'm weak. I'm a failure. Why can't I control this? Just get up and move, Barb. Please just get up. I can't. What will Mickey think of me, sitting in the corner of the sofa?

❏

He was kind. He said he'd been waiting for this to happen, but I didn't trust him, certain his patience would be limited. I had no reservations about the unconditional love of our cat, Buster. When Mickey came home from work in the evenings, Buster would hear the garage door open and rush from our bedroom where he spent the day curled on my pillow. He would find me trapped on the family room sofa and jump into my lap, quickly settle in and rest his paw on my hand. I wondered if Buster didn't trust Mickey either.

I was afraid of turning into a lady with pink fuzzy slippers and a ratty bathrobe who sat with the remote control in one hand and a Twinkie in the other. If I weren't doing something, I had no value. I was defective. I couldn't believe there was integrity in just "being." I was convinced that if I heard voices, they would tell me what to do to change the world. They wouldn't tell me to sit on the sofa. They would call me to action, not insist that I rest. To soothe myself I recalled the philosopher who said, "I think, therefore I am." He didn't say, "I think, therefore I stay as busy as possible, striving to reach my goals and fulfill my affirmations of working, raising a family, volunteering for just causes, and taking yoga classes."

On good days, I felt my soul just had to get away for a while and had left a sign around my neck, "Gone fishing."

Most days were bad. I wanted my therapist to tell me exactly what to do to fix myself and exactly how long it would take. I wanted her to give me a process and a timetable. Of course, she couldn't.

As I struggled with my present, Lani struggled with her future. She also went to a few sessions with a therapist in Amherst who told her she was very good at knowing how to be happy but not good at all when it came to knowing how to be sad.

"What bullshit," Mickey said.

But I knew it wasn't. I was beginning to understand that her anger was a replacement for the sadness she didn't want to acknowledge, just as my sadness held the anger I couldn't express. So she raged, and I cried. What a pair we were. I wished I had been able to pass on to my daughter the ability to honor her whole self, her sadness as well as her joy, but I couldn't because it was something I had never learned. I was fueled by the dictates of being nice and often abandoned myself in order to accommodate others. Some people believe, and I was taught, that this is the correct and proper way to behave. Now I can't think of anything more dangerous or damaging, and I wonder if I will ever find the parts of me I have forsaken. After all these years, how can I begin to honor myself? I don't know. Maybe sitting on the sofa is a beginning.

So I sat. And to avoid thinking about myself, I wondered about my daughter and what lay ahead for her. Would her relationship with Scott survive this trauma? Would they stay together? Or would this be the love remembered with a sigh and a smile?

What about school? She wanted to be an occupational therapist. Could she get into a graduate school or were there prereq-
uisite classes? Which school? Near Scott? Near family? And
more immediately, what would she do in a few weeks when her
coaching job was over and her apartment lease was up?

Lani phoned one morning to let me know she'd decided to fly
to Albuquerque and spend a year with Shira. She felt good
about the decision, but she was anxious about packing up and
moving four years of accumulated college life. What would she
store at home and how would she ship those things to
Minnesota? What did she want with her at Shira's, and how
would she get all those belongings on the plane?

"This is too aggravating," she snapped. "I don't want to make
all these arrangements. What a pain. If I had a car, I could pack
everything in it and just drive home, unload some stuff, see you
and Dad, then drive to Shira's. I could travel at my own pace,
not have to worry about getting to airports on time. Okay!
That's it! I've got some money saved. I'm going to buy a car
now. Bye!" She hung up.

I looked at the phone. Most women I know buy a pair of
shoes when they're depressed.

The next day, she told us that she bought a 1984 Chevy
Celebrity for a thousand dollars. She was packing it with her
belongings and would drive from Boston to Minneapolis. If
the car made it that far, she'd take it all the way to
Albuquerque. She refused to be on a schedule and didn't know
when she'd reach home: two or three days, five or six days, as
long as it took. It was not a journey to be measured in miles
or hours, but in pages journaled, tears shed, and drives across
open fields while fingers tapped on the steering wheel to the
rhythm of a favorite tape, fresh air blowing through the open
car window.

It was a good plan for her but not for me. Once more, I had
to wait for word that my daughter was safe. Please call, I mumbled at night into my pillow. But she never did.

Four days later, early in the evening, the doorbell rang and Lani stood outside, grinning. She had a golden tan and looked healthy and strong. The scars on her throat and arm were beginning to fade, and her hair had grown back. There were screams and hugs and kisses. Mickey and I ran to help unload her car as the gray sky began to drizzle. The maroon Chevy was built like a tank and it rested in our driveway, old, but solid. Through the car windows, we saw empty cans of Dr. Pepper lying on a dashboard totally covered with torn candy wrappers, Reese's Peanut Butter Cups being the standout favorite. Cardboard boxes were piled to the roof in the back seat. The guitar Scott had given her was in the front seat. So were a pillow and two blankets and more boxes. When she opened the trunk, I was ready to duck, expecting a cartoon explosion of shorts and shirts flying through the air, jeans landing on the grass, underpants catching on the branches of a tree. My instincts were right. An explosion was coming, but it wouldn't be clothing that went flying.

There was tremendous tension between Lani and me, and it seemed that despite all that had happened, I might still lose her somehow. We needed a good talk. I didn't know how to begin but Lani did. She and I were driving to my folks for dinner in thick slow rush-hour traffic, and she let loose without preamble.

"You're too nice to me," she shouted. "The nicer you are, the meaner I get. Then you're nice to me again and I get even meaner. I see myself doing it, and I can't stop." Her anger felt like an airbag instantly exploding into the car. "I know I am pushing you away, but you have to stop being so nice. Don't give me special treatment!"

My hands tightened on the steering wheel, my jaw clenched, my stomach knotted. I can do that.

We reached my parents apartment and were waiting in the entryway to get buzzed in.

"You were afraid for me driving home alone, weren't you?" she snapped.

You can't imagine.

"Well, I was, too, but danger is always a possibility; we just have never been so aware of it. I know you're afraid I'll get hurt again."

You have no idea.

It wasn't much of a conversation. I didn't know how to defend myself, and before I had time to recover we were sitting at my folks' dining room table passing platters of chicken, commenting on the weather and the traffic, and complimenting the chef.

Lani told us about her morning with Mickey's ninety-two-year-old mother, Baubie. Baubie's sight was failing, and, today, Lani had driven her to an eye doctor appointment.

"We talked about losing our sight and we agreed that those things aren't a tragedy. They're a part of life. We can decide how we'll deal with them and then move on."

Move on. Could I move on?

I thought I had. I didn't object when Lani moved back to Amherst only three and a half months after her accident. I didn't argue when she drove home from Boston alone. But as I considered it more closely, I realize I hadn't moved on at all. It was impossible because my feet were planted deeply in the ground, heels dug in, arms aching from holding the invisible cord that I had wrapped around my daughter. I was trying hard, too hard, to be a good mother, to be everything she needed. But now I was weary deep into my bones. I couldn't do it any longer. That night, I took off my Australian ring for the first time and set it gently on my dresser.

Lani made the journey from Minneapolis to Albuquerque and I sighed with relief. Soon, she had a full schedule of waitressing, volunteering at a hospital, and studying for her graduate school entrance exams. She napped when she needed to and still found time to do a little jogging, a little horseback riding. She even took a dance class from her sister.

The phone calls from Albuquerque were much easier to handle than the calls from Boston. "I'm so nervous about studying for the grad school entrance exams. What if I can't remember everything I'm cramming into my head?"

"You'll do great," I said, totally confident.

A few days later, "Guess what happened to me today? I was riding my bike home from school and you know how I can't see anything on my left side, and, well, I rode right into one of those big garbage containers and flew off my bike!"

My stomach tightened. Afraid to ask if she had hurt herself, I responded nonchalantly as possible, "Ohhhh. Really."

"Really! My hands and knees are skinned, and I'm going to be a little stiff. I'm sure glad I was wearing my helmet."

Me, too. When our conversation ended, I hung up the phone and stared into space, acutely aware that the world is under no obligation to protect my daughter. *This is so hard.*

The following week, another call came. I was ready.

"Mom, Shira and I want to tell you something."

Oh, no, what?

"It's really important." She was building up to something.

I can handle this.

"Well," she took a deep breath, "We made a checklist for the perfect husband, and the first three qualifications are the ability to speak English, a valid driver's license, and no felony record!" I laughed so quickly that it came out as a gasp. *Maybe this won't be so bad after all.*

❑

Mickey and I visited the girls at the end of July. Shira had moved out of the back of her studio and into a small town-house. Most of the furniture was gathered from flea markets: a sofa with orange and blue floral designs, a wooden rocking chair, a scratched coffee table with permanent ring marks from sweating glasses. There were familiar photos scattered on homemade bookshelves, and a lamp from our basement. Shira was just finishing a summer workshop with high school students, part of Albuquerque's Arts in the City program. She'd never worked with such a large group of adolescents before and apologized to me often for her behavior as a teenager. "I don't know how I acted in high school, Mom. But if this is how teenagers act, I'm so sorry. I had no idea!"

Ah, vindication!

Mickey and I spent two days with the girls, taking them to dinner, curling up with them on the sofa, and watching videos, playing board games, and soaking up their presence.

As a gift to myself I had made arrangements to go horseback riding in Taos where a family on the Pueblo Indian Reservation ran a small ranch and guided people on horseback into the sacred mountains. I planned to leave early Sunday afternoon and spend the evening in Taos because my ride was scheduled for 7:00 A.M. Monday morning. Not wanting me to take the three-hour drive alone, Mickey decided to come along even though he had a bad cold. He buckled himself into the passenger seat coughing and blowing his nose, while I adjusted the rearview mirror and Shira gave me final instructions about driving her car. "This car is old, and the engine is tired."

It sounds like me!

"So don't go over fifty-five miles per hour, and don't turn on the air conditioning, and call me when you get settled into your motel so I know you arrived safely."

Ho ho ho. The mother-daughter roles are reversing!

I followed Shira's instructions, so our trip was hot and slow. It felt right that I be driving since this was my adventure, but I know it frustrated Mickey not to be in control. The drive was glorious. Each curve in the road exposed a new piece of brilliant blue sky and rugged mountains. One curve suddenly put the mountains at our back and shifted our journey onto a flat, vast desert. Sand and sun blew in the open car windows until we reached a landmark on the outskirts of Taos.

The gorge wasn't visible until we were at its edge. It appeared as unexpectedly in the desert as the desert had from the mountains. It was a place where the Earth had ripped apart violently eons ago. A bridge spanning the gorge let us look down to the Rio Grande River, a silver ribbon seven-hundred-feet below. In the late afternoon, small white birds flew in the cool shadows of the rocky walls. This is a hard land full of violent and unexpected changes. And it is so beautiful.

It's trying to teach you something, Barb.

❏

I called the ranch to confirm my riding time and was asked if I could come out before settling in for the evening.

"There are releases that need to be signed," explained the cheerful woman who answered the phone. "And besides, we'd love to meet you and your husband."

The ranch was off a dirt road, ten minutes from our motel. The small corral held five horses, and the rambler-style house was shaded by tall trees. In the front of the house was the ranch office.

Sandy rose from behind her desk to greet us. She was a large woman with long, blond hair and a warm smile. Her husband entered a few minutes later and introduced himself as Storm Star. Sandy laughed. "He is full-blooded Pueblo Indian, the Red Willow People, and when I met him in California I thought he was Italian!"

As we visited, they asked casually about my background and riding experience. They were trying to get a sense of me, checking me out. Would I be a timid rider who, at the last minute, refused to walk my horse out of their front yard? Or would I be the crazed lady who, once mounted, kicked my horse violently and went galloping off into the sunset? I hoped to convince them that even though it had been a long time, I still remembered how to do this. In bed that night, I tossed fitfully, like a child the night before the first day of school. While Mickey slept in, I arrived back at the ranch promptly at 7:00 A.M. Storm Star was saddling our horses and didn't want to talk. I couldn't tell if he was being the silent contemplative Indian or needed a strong cup of black coffee.

After we mounted, I was content to ride quietly alongside him as we jogged down a dirt road with two dogs from the ranch following us. We cut across an open field of tall grass and began winding up the side of the mountain, following no path that I could see, slowly rising into cooler air. The tall grass was replaced by bushes, replaced by fragile trees that became towering evergreens. We had gone up from desert to forest. Coyotes yipped and howled, and the dogs leapt into the thick trees for a chase.

We stopped three times during our climb. Each time, Storm Star turned his horse to face me. "Whatever fears you need to release, you can do so now."

It was so big here, so open. A safe place to let things go where they couldn't bounce off a wall and slam back into me. They had room to blow away. At the third stop, I realized it wasn't fear that caused my ache, but grief.

Storm Star looked at me calmly. "Your daughter has returned. It is not grief, but joy, that overwhelms you and needs to be let loose." Does that make any sense? Could I be overwhelmed with joy? I suppose. Joy can bring tears to my eyes and take my breath away. Storm Star turned and continued riding up the mountain. I followed and as my horse carried me along, I cried.

We reached an opening in the trees and dismounted to rest our horses. My tears had dried and I took in the view of the valley below. "That thin, dark line running across the desert is the gorge," Storm Star explained. "The grouping of trees on the mountain side to our right protects our sacred lake."

Maybe someday I can go there.

Storm Star stretched out his arm. "At one time, this was all underwater." He bent down and picked up a rock and handed it to me. No, not a rock. A fossilized sea shell. A seashell from a mountain top. My gift from the mountain. Is this a hustle? Did he plant this yesterday for us to find today? Who would expect to find a seashell on a mountain top, waiting to be discovered countless millenia after the water receded. I wondered what unexpected treasures I might find waiting for me in my sacred places.

Our ride down the mountain was fast. When we reached flat land, we cantered across a field of yellow flowers. Storm Star stopped again, broke off a piece of bush, and handed it to me. Sage. I inhaled the scent and smiled.

As we neared the end of the ride, we let the horses walk to cool down. It was almost 10:00 A.M. when we reached the ranch. I was tired and sore and happy. Sandy was standing outside and invited me into the office for coffee and a muffin. I sat and stretched out my legs. My plan was to break off small pieces of the muffin and graciously nibble on little bits at a time, but before I could stop myself I took three big bites and the entire treat was gone.

Sandy and I talked and laughed. We shared stories about our children and our plans for the rest of the summer. Then she suddenly became very serious. "I need to tell you something. I wasn't sure I should, but I think it's the right thing to do and you will take it in the spirit offered."

"Of course I will. And now you've got me really curious."

"When you and your husband were both here yesterday I saw something in your husband. Sometimes I can do that, see things in people. I saw something in your husband. I hope that doesn't sound too crazy."

"No, I think it's an extraordinary gift. I am grateful that you think I'm a safe enough person to share that kind of information with."

She nodded. "Barbara, I see sickness around him."

"I know. He's had a really bad cold lately that he just can't seem to shake."

"It's more than that. It's deep inside. I wanted you to know. I felt you would understand."

"I don't know what to say. Thank you for telling me."

I didn't want to hear any more so I looked at my watch and set down my coffee cup. "Oh, I didn't realize how late it was. I'd better get going. Thank you again for everything."

Sandy sighed as she stood. I sensed she was disappointed that I didn't understand the gravity of her message. But she gave me a strong hug, wished me well, and told me to return again anytime. On my drive back to the motel I made a mental note to tell Mickey he should call his doctor for a complete checkup when we got back to Minneapolis, assuming the sickness Sandy saw was physical.

When I returned to our room for a quick shower, Mickey said he was feeling better and offered to drive back to Albuquerque. I agreed. I wanted to close my eyes and think about my morning. I didn't have an epiphany. There was no revelation, no booming voice. Not even a still, small one. But I wanted to believe there had been a shift in my spirit, maybe from the mountain, maybe from deep inside me. Wherever it came from, I was sure it was ancient and had been waiting patiently.

It was very romantic to think I'd ridden into the sacred mountains and come down from them healed. The pain in my hip was fading, and I took that as a sign that it was time to move forward. But I wasn't finished looking back. As hard as I tried to ignore it, dismiss it, my heart still ached. It was in my heart that I dug a trench those first days in the hospital. Staying in that trench for so long, I had begun stumbling over dark shapes deep in the shadows. What was happening? Had I come across wounded pieces of myself, buried pains I thought were gone, sorrows I thought had dissolved? I was frightened. I was not finding lovely seashells. I was finding mangled bodies.

By the end of the summer, I was making lists compulsively. My schedule for the day. My errands: the post office, the bank, the drug store. The work to be done: Mary Kay customers to call, orders to fill, meetings to plan. The same list over and over. I was also compulsive about making sure lights were off and doors were locked. When I returned home from any outing, I had to check phone messages immediately. What if something happened while I was gone? Reading newspaper articles about accidents made me cry. Being with people was exhausting. It was stressful to follow a conversation, and I would worry all night that I had said the wrong thing or had made a comment that could be misconstrued.

I slept a lot, a quilt pulled up to my chin, the cat lying protectively next to me. It was not restful. It was like going into hiding. I was functioning in slow motion as if I were under water. Emptying the dishwasher was a huge effort. So was changing the sheets on the bed. And taking a shower was a two-step process. I had to push myself to get in, and then force myself to get out, sometimes not remembering if I had shampooed my hair or simply gotten it wet.

I limped along a day at a time until suddenly it was the eve of Rosh Hashanah, the Jewish New Year, the first anniversary of the accident. And then it was the ten days between Rosh Hashanah and Yom Kippur. The days we waited and watched and prayed. I hadn't realized how long these ten days had been. I curled up on the sofa as often as I could. I was so scared. Of everything. I couldn't move.

I dreaded the promise I had made Mickey to leave on a vacation with him the day after Yom Kippur. How could I have made that commitment? It had happened in April after hearing Lani had received her clean bill of health. I was thrilled my daughter was healed. Of course a vacation would be great. Lani was safe. I could have fun now. So Mickey had planned a two-week road trip out West visiting cousins and ultimately arriving in Whitefish, Montana, on the western edge of Glacier National Park, where he needed to attend a judges' conference.

I didn't want to get off the sofa, let alone leave my house. And road trips were never my favorite vacation. Driving through Colorado three years ago, Mickey took the car up a narrow, unpaved mountain road with a steep drop-off and no guard rail. For twenty minutes, I had gripped the armrest with white knuckles and screamed at him to slow down. He never did. And it never occurred to me to get out of the car in the middle of nowhere, on the edge of the mountain road.

Mickey assured me nothing like that would happen again as he packed me into the front seat of the car with a container of Pringles, three bagels, and a large jar of cranberry juice.

The first day, we got through South Dakota. My mood matched the scenery, flat and gray. The second day, we entered Wyoming and, as the week went by, we drove into Idaho and then Montana. The scenery was breathtaking. Mountains. Rivers. Forests. More mountains. We stopped in small towns. Dubois, Wyoming. Filer, Idaho. Darby, Montana. We saw places with familiar names. Jackson Hole. Sun Valley.

We visited cousins we hadn't seen in years. Diane was a single mom raising two teenage daughters. She lived a simple life in a small town. From her apartment, she could see the beauty shop where she worked and the high school her girls attended. Outside her patio was a single oak tree. From her bedroom, she could hear water as it trickled through a culvert below her window. Gary lived with his wife and two children in a huge, sprawling home in the mountains, dense with forest. His family could sit by the massive fireplace in their living room and, through the floor-to-ceiling windows, watch a rushing stream as it ran around the edge of the house. These lifestyles were so different. One seemed so small and the other so large. My first instinct was to assume that bigger was better. But it's not; it's just bigger. Then I realized these two people had decided how they wanted to live and had chosen what felt right for them. Did I have the courage to make such decisions?

In Sun Valley, we visited a thriving art gallery. Twenty years ago, the owner had visited the area, fallen in love with the rolling mountains, and decided to stay. With no source of income, she bought herself a book on art and taught herself how to paint. In Montana, we went to a dude ranch and met a woman who had quit her job in Cincinnati as a high-powered attorney five years earlier so she could clean stalls, feed horses, and help run the barn. At the judges' conference, there was a woman who had been a single teenage mother, put herself through law school, and was now chief judge of a juvenile court. Another woman judge was the first in her family to ever graduate high school. The scenery of the human spirit was breathtaking. When Mickey and I returned to Minneapolis, these women came with me, whispering in my ear, watching over my shoulder.

They rejoiced as I made another attempt to begin horseback riding. And my friend, Ann, was thrilled that her constant encouragement over lunches and during phone calls had finally paid off. I drove to Dreamfield Farms, a barn specializing in show jumping, my passion. When the trainer put me on a big, dark horse named Humphrey, I knew I was home, and I felt the smiles of these sister spirits. By following their hearts, they had given me permission to do the same. During my first lesson, I trotted around the ring once and had to stop to catch my breath. By the end of the hour, I was trotting over a very small jump and I couldn't stop grinning. I grinned all the way home.

I can't believe that, after all these years, I'm doing this again!

After my second lesson, I cried all the way home.

I can't believe that, after all these years, I'm doing this again!

During the third lesson, my horse spooked, spun, and dumped me in the dirt. It happened so fast I didn't have time to get scared, and I didn't get hurt.

There's another lesson here, Barb.

A month later, I was offered the opportunity to lease a horse. He wouldn't officially be mine, but by sharing the expenses, I could also share the riding. His name was Sparky because he was very quiet and gentle and didn't spark much at all unless you brought him carrots or apples or his favorite, Kellogg's Cracklin' Oat Bran cereal. Then he shook and nodded his big head, or tapped his hoof, insisting he was wonderful and therefore needed to be fed immediately.

I couldn't even consider saying no to this offer, but I didn't want history to repeat itself. And what history would that be? My husband discounting my passion. Feeling forced to give up something I love. I thought of the dream I shared with Lani, when I believed the horse represented a vital piece of myself. If Mickey never respected that part of me, does that mean he has no respect for what is vital in me, for my essence, for my unique spark? That would be so painful. Unbearable. I didn't listen for the answer to that question. I wasn't prepared to hear it. But I agreed to the lease and decided it was time I learned to honor myself.

I was taking a big step and, for security, I continued retreating to the sofa when I needed to hide, even though covering myself with the afghan didn't keep me safe from the voices.

"You're trying to honor yourself! Ha! You're weak, you're lazy, you have no self-discipline, and good grief, what are you still doing on the sofa? Get over it!"

Sadly, I believed all I heard, but my body was wiser than my mind and it wouldn't move. A dear friend called during this episode and spoke to me gently. "I hear voices like that, too. I have tried to ignore them. I have tried to yell at them to shut up. It doesn't work. Now I simply thank them for their input and tell them that I must disagree. Please remember," she told me, "that there is only one voice to listen to. It is the voice of compassion and love. It is the true voice of God, Angels, the Universe, the Great Spirit, whatever name you want to give it. It may be hard to hear over the other racket, but it is the only voice you need."

I did my best to follow her instructions and began to hear the whispers: "I love you. I'll protect you. You are strong. You are wonderful. I believe in you." They were the words I spoke to Lani when she was in her coma. The same words exactly.

I listened carefully to those words, especially after I was told that our Australian attorney requested that Lani return to Brisbane to undergo a battery of doctors' exams, so her legal case could settle faster. What am I going to do when she leaves?

Pray every day: God bless and protect my children. Is that enough? Can't I do something stronger? Maybe if I kneel while I pray or rub stones together I can be more effective. Faith and fear keep bumping into each other as they race around in my head like crazed children in bumper cars. When will this all be over?

CHAPTER Ten

Monday, August 7, 2000

Lani left on the trip that had been interrupted by her accident almost two years earlier. Her starting point this time was San Diego, where she visited Scott, who was now training with the Coast Guard. Their romance had dissolved over the past year, and Scott and Lani were doing their best to stay good friends.

After a week in San Diego, Lani met Emily in Los Angeles and they flew together to Australia for doctors' appointments, the same procedures Patrick had gone through just a month earlier. Emily would stay for the checkups and then return home, but Lani decided to keep traveling. The insurance company reimbursed the girls' travel expenses back to Australia and our attorney offered his home, so they didn't need a hotel.

Lani's first stop was the Royal Brisbane Hospital where she visited the 4B/ICU and the open ward of 2B. She got hugs from nurses and therapists who recognized her immediately and treated her like a celebrity. She was disappointed when she couldn't find Dr. D'urso and was told that he had been transferred to a hospital in Sydney.

Outside the ICU, Lani paused to speak to a woman sitting alone on the bench. "Don't give up hope. I'm a miracle that came out of that ward." She turned to walk away, but the woman called her back explaining that she had three children at home and was frantically waiting for news about her husband, the doctors not being optimistic. The two sat on the bench, talking for over an hour. Lani was humbled by the gift she had been given: not just the gift of life, but the gift of hope that she could offer others.

After her week of medical exams was over, she celebrated by snorkeling on the Great Barrier Reef, sailing the Whit Sunday Islands, visiting Lorraine and her six children, and going to a barbeque with two new friends, Shorty and Liam, the paramedics who were first on the scene of the accident. Then she was off to Thailand, where she rode elephants into the jungle and swam in blue pools under pristine waterfalls. Next, it was Morocco, where she visited her friend Ann in the Peace Corps.

While Lani traveled, I was on my own adventure, going to the barn two or three times a week. It kept me distracted, and it kept me exhausted. Riding is hard work and I got stronger physically. Jumping horses is not easy, and I made a lot of mistakes—reminders that mistakes are acceptable, necessary, human. What I remember most vividly, more than the riding itself, were the times after lessons on hot summer days when I would wash down Sparky and lead him out to an open field to eat grass. He would drop his head and bury his nose in the sweet, green lawn. I would lean against his shoulder with my arm over his back. I would wonder, after all that had happened, how was I different? Is it possible to have gone through such intense trauma and have no revelation or transformation? Hard as I tried, I didn't see one. Maybe I was simply more of myself than I had been before—myself in greater depth.

And that was the result of an excavation, not a revelation. In the darkness I had traveled, I had found abandoned pieces of myself and gently carried them with me when I came back into the light. If it were not for the accident, I may have never gone into that place and would have been forever scattered, separated. There are more pieces to find and a lifetime of searching, but this is a beginning.

And my family, how have they changed? When Lani returns from her travels she will be packing up her belongings in Albuquerque and returning to Boston to study occupational therapy at Tufts University. Shira's dance company is blossoming. Her programs are changing lives and being recognized nationally for the difference they are making in the community.

That's what they're doing, moving on boldly. But I can't see the private shifts they've made to accommodate this tremendous experience. I picture the concrete foundation of a home suddenly cracked open. This split can't be repaired, and a choice has to be made. Do you throw an area rug over the spot and try not to trip over it, or do you celebrate the space, planting flowers in the earth that has miraculously appeared? I believe my girls are the gardening type.

What about Mickey? I don't see a change in him. I do notice the crack in the foundation has caused a door to unlatch, to creak open. It's a secret door to a secret room. The room is Mickey's, and I don't want to look inside. I love Mickey, the tender Mickey who holds my hand and makes me laugh, who forgets his keys, who makes pancakes on Sunday mornings. And I believe Mickey loves me. So I don't look, but the door remains open.

EPILOGUE

Wednesday, September 26, 2001

It has been three years since the accident and three years to the day since Lani's first complicated surgery. It is Kol Nidre, the eve before the Jewish Day of Atonement. Again, just as it was three years ago, Mickey is not with me. This time, it's my choice. I'm sitting on my sofa in my cozy second-floor apartment. The patio door is opened, and I can hear the suburban traffic of people coming home from work. It's sunny, in the sixties. There is an evergreen tree in front of my little patio that gives me some privacy. It's a two-bedroom apartment. I wanted the second bedroom for my Mary Kay office and a for a hide-a-bed, hoping one or both of my daughters will come for a visit. Our house is sold, orange counter tops and all. And I have left Mickey. Once doors to secret rooms have been opened, their contents are bound to seep out.

I do understand why people don't leave. Change is hard. Many of us get upset when regular programming is interrupted on TV or when the grocery store moves the cereal to a different aisle. Mickey's room showed me there was no promise of happily ever after. Lani's accident proved there was no guarantee of safety. But Lani recovered, and so would I. Like my daughter, I would push to heal the broken parts of my life. It is Kol Nidre and another life has been saved. Mine.

I'm in a place that wouldn't feel safe to many people, alone after thirty years of marriage. I've never lived on my own, other than six months in college with a household of other girls. I don't feel alone. Single is a better word. I wonder if my husband ever loved me. I don't think it was in him. I worry that my life has been a lie for all these years. But I wasn't lying. He was.

There are days I come home from running errands, unlock my apartment door, drop my purse on the table and sigh, "I'm fifty-three years old and I'm living alone in this little apartment." Most mornings, though, I get up, open the blinds, look out on the evergreen tree, stretch, rub my head, and proclaim, "I'm fifty-three years old and I'm living alone in this little apartment!"

❑

During my nine-month lease, I would meet with mediators and divorce attorneys. Shira would become engaged to Rick, a wonderful man, and we would plan a wedding. A month before the wedding, I would purchase and move into a small town-house. I rushed at these projects, determined that they only looked big, just as Lani had taught me. She would graduate with her master's degree in occupational therapy and return to Minneapolis to do a three-month internship at North Memorial with the women who treated her when she was a patient there.

My life became breathtaking. I felt like I was at a shopping mall the day before Christmas. It was a colorful rushing, on the edge of being out of control. My parents would call to see how I was doing and my mother would say, "You are strong. You are brave. I believe in you. I love you."

Before I knew it, Lani had decided to go on yet another adventure. She met a friend on the West Coast and bicycled from

Vancouver to Mexico, nearly two thousand miles. She was gone for ten weeks. I did my best to worry less and trust more. It was not a sign of wisdom, but of exhaustion. When Lani returned to Minneapolis, it was to gather up her belongings and go back to Massachusetts yet again. She stayed with me while she was getting ready for her trip back East. The night before she left, I got into my pajamas, and Lani got into the T-shirt she used as pajamas. I made us hot chocolate, and we climbed onto my bed with our steaming mugs.

I sat propped up with pillows, resting my head against the wall, the cat settled by my feet. Lani lay on her stomach, holding her mug in front of her.

"Mom, you know one of the things I decide to do with my occupational therapy degree?"

"No. What?"

"I decided to do therapy with horses."

"I didn't think horses needed therapy! Haha!"

"No, Mom!" She punched me lightly on the arm. "Therapy using horses. Patients can get on the horses and the riding is their therapy, and it's really effective. Even if they just work around the horses. It can make a big difference."

"Lani, what a great thing to do."

"Speaking of making a difference, Mom, do you think you'll date again?"

"Someday. How weird will that be?"

We giggled.

"I can't believe I'm going back to Boston tomorrow. Would you like me to check in with you each night while I'm on the road?"

"That would be wonderful."

I was fading. Lani took my cup, tucked me in, kissed me good night, and turned off the light. "I love you, Mom."

"I love you, too."

I lay in bed, smiling in the quiet night.